THE
1 HOUR
CHINA
CONSUMER BOOK

FIVE SHORT STORIES
THAT EXPLAIN THE BRUTAL
FIGHT FOR ONE BILLION
CONSUMERS

JEFFREY TOWSON
JONATHAN WOETZEL

ISBN-10: 099144504X (paperback)
ISBN-13: 978-0-9914450-4-2 (paperback)

Version 2015.02.21

10 9 8 7 6 5 4 3 2 1

CONTENTS

PRAISE FOR ONE HOUR CHINA

"Without question the best 60 minutes you will spend on China."

Jonathan Anderson
Emerging Markets Advisors

"For most people, the intellectual return on time spent reading this book is almost unrivaled."

Value Walk

"This quick, fascinating book will give readers who know little or nothing about doing business in China - everything they need to know or remember about how to succeed in business in China. One hour with this book will make you an expert on business in China."

Dick Gephardt
Majority-Minority Leader
U.S. House of Representatives
1989-2002

"The One Hour China Book offers an even-handed and well-illustrated insight into the seemingly chaotic and often self-contradictory China prospects in a pleasantly easy read."

Rui-Gang Li
Chairman, China Media Capital

"This book simplifies China in a very elegant and smart way. These distinguished authors tell you clearly what you most need to know right now."

James McGregor
Author of One Billion Customers: Lessons from the Front Lines of Doing Business in China

"The superlatives typically used to describe China's economic rise over the past two decades fail to do justice to its historic significance. In their refreshing speed-read of a book, Jonathan Woetzel and Jeffrey Towson take a simpler approach and let the facts speak for themselves. In doing so they capture, clearly and concisely, the magnitude of China's transformation."

Tom Mitchell
Beijing Correspondent, Financial Times

"I heartily recommend this volume. It succinctly describes the six megatrends reshaping Chinese society today and does so in an engaging and thoroughly enjoyable fashion. As a faculty member who also likes to tackle huge subjects and distill them to their essence, I congratulate the two authors for their effort. The book makes for essential reading on your next trip to China."

Lawton Robert Burns, Ph.D.
James Joo-Jin Kim Professor
Chair, Health Care Management Department
Director, Wharton Center for Health Management and Economics
University of Pennsylvania

"This beguiling book manages to boil an enormous amount of complexity down into a fully digestible capsule compendium that is centered around a series of "mega-trends" that are exemplified by actual Chinese entrepreneurs and their concrete businesses. As such, it is both a very accessible and fascinating tour of contemporary Chinese business, and of China itself."

Orville Schell
Arthur Ross Director, Center on US-China Relations, Asia Society, New York City and co-author of "Wealth and Power: China's Long March to the 21st Century."

ALSO BY THE AUTHORS

The One Hour China Book: Two Peking University Professors Explain All of China Business in Six Short Stories, by Jeffrey Towson and Jonathan Woetzel (March 2014)

What Would Ben Graham Do Now? A New Value Investing Playbook for a Global Age, by Jeffrey Towson (May 21, 2011)

Operation China: From Strategy to Execution, by Jimmy Hexter and Jonathan Woetzel (December 18, 2007)

Capitalist China: Strategies for a Revolutionized Economy, by Jonathan Woetzel (August 13, 2003)

FIVE SHORT STORIES THAT EXPLAIN THE BRUTAL FIGHT FOR CHINESE CONSUMERS

In November 2007, the Milwaukee Bucks played the Houston Rockets at the Houston Toyota Center. It really wasn't a very good basketball game. And it wasn't at all consequential for the teams or the NBA. It ended with an unexciting rout of the Bucks, 104-88.

What was consequential about that particular game was that it was the first time Chinese basketball star Yao Ming, then on the Rockets, had played against rising Chinese star Yi Jianlian, then on the Bucks. And that is why approximately 200M Chinese tuned in to watch.

To put those 200M viewers in perspective, in 2012 the most watched American sporting event was the Super

Bowl, which attracted only 112M viewers. And that was its biggest viewership in 26 years.

We don't actually know exactly how many people watched that NBA game. Most estimates put the viewership at 200M to 250M people. But we do know that the Yao-Yi game was shown on 19 networks in China, including CCTV-5, Guangdong TV, Guangzhou TV, and ESPN Star Sports. We can comfortably conclude viewership was massive.

Chinese fans waiting for NBA star LeBron James at a Nike store in Guangzhou
(photo by ImagineChina)

That's a good story to keep in mind when thinking about Chinese consumers. It's one thing to talk about one billion consumers far away. It's another when 200M of them decide to watch a basketball game in Houston. It's unexpected. It's a bit overwhelming. And it has lots of unusual consequences, such as the joke (at that time) that if you're a basketball player and you want a shoe deal with Nike, you try to stand close to Yao Ming when the cameras are on.

We are at the beginning of the Chinese consumer century. And that 2007 game is a good official starting point. Not only was the viewership stunning, but it was for a basketball game, something Chinese have never really played and didn't much care about 20 years ago. So basketball is a good symbol for both the scale of rising Chinese consumers and how unpredictable they can be.

But there's a problem with that type of "wow" China consumer story: Big consumer numbers are at best half the story. And it can make you very naïve about rising Chinese consumers. Here's a better story to remember.

Robert Ravens is an Australian farmer and the creator of the "Bobbie Bear". He lives on a remote Tasmanian farm and uses excess lavender from his fields to make bright purple teddy bears. The lavender is stuffed into the bears along with some wheat and a heat pack. The fragrant teddy bears can then be heated in a microwave, which apparently makes them nice to sleep with. He mostly sold his Bobbie Bears online and in his farm's gift shop.

However, in mid-2013, a young Chinese celebrity named Zhang Xinyu posted a picture of herself on her Weibo account hugging her Bobbie Bear. This went viral and apparently caused young women across China to go crazy. They began to flood Mr. Ravens' small Tasmanian farm with teddy bear orders.

Overwhelmed, Mr. Ravens had to stop taking Internet orders. He then had to stop taking phone, email or pre-orders. Someone even hacked into his website to place teddy bear orders in his system. And then, finally, he had to start limiting bears sold in his gift shop to one per visitor, as Chinese tourists were somehow finding their way to his Northwestern Australian farm in droves. Visitors to the farm exceeded 60,000 annually and each bear that was finished was immediately rushed to the gift store. In 2014, Chinese president Xi Jinping was even presented with a Bobbie Bear upon his arrival at the Tasmania airport. All of this was likely not what Mr. Ravens envisioned when he bought the run-down farm in 2007 as a retirement project.

At first glance, this is similar to the NBA story. Surging Chinese demand with unexpected and entertaining consequences. However, within weeks of the Bobbie Bear phenomenon, shops across China began offering copycat purple bears. And soon hundreds of thousands of copycats were being sold online and then resold throughout China. Mr. Ravens responded by issuing authentication numbers for his bears so people could tell if they had the real thing.

And then a few months later, the Chinese government jumped in. Some of the fake bears had bugs in their stuffing (definitely not lavender) and the government issued a ban on all lavender bears, including the original Bobbie Bears.

This, in many ways, is the real story of rising Chinese consumers. Yes, Chinese consumers are a big economic phenomenon. But the competition for them can be very fast and utterly ruthless. And hovering in the background of all this is the Chinese government, which frequently intervenes as an active player – and sometimes a competitor. "Consumers plus competition plus government" is a better description of what is really going on. The fight for one billion Chinese consumers is really about the shifting interaction of these three factors. And that is what this book is about.

OUR OBSESSION WITH "ONE HOUR CHINA" BOOKS

This book is a follow-up to The One Hour China Book: Two Peking University Professors Explain All of China Business in Six Short Stories. It became a best-seller and we became big believers in focused, "speed reads". In a world of limited time but unlimited content, we have found the one-hour constraint to be invaluable. It forces us to delete 90% of our writing and to present you with only our very best thinking.

If we have done our job well, you should be able finish this in an hour (not counting the Appendices) and have a valuable set of frameworks for this topic. Most Chinese consumer headlines (say, in the Wall Street Journal) should make sense to you.

"Rising Chinese Consumers" is also one of the six China mega-trends we outlined in our first book (shown below).

In that book, we argued these mega-trends are like tectonic plates moving underneath the surface of China. If you can understand them, the chaos of activity on the surface (and in the headlines) becomes a lot more understandable.

The 6 China Megatrends

All of these mega-trends are long-term economic phenomena, typically lasting decades. They are fueling the revenues of large companies and have given rise to many of China's most famous billionaires. Within these, urbanization and rising Chinese consumers are arguably the most long-term and fundamental. Although, the Chinese Internet tends to get the most press.

ABOUT US

We both live and work with one foot in China and one foot in the West. Our careers are in management consulting (Jonathan) and private equity (Jeff). But we also write and teach at business schools a good portion of our time.

Jonathan is a senior partner at McKinsey in Shanghai. He has spent +20 years running hundreds (thousands?) of CEO-level consulting engagements across China and was basically the guy who opened McKinsey's Shanghai office in 1994. Jeff refers to him as the "national archive of China business", which Jonathan was unaware of prior to reading this paragraph.

Jonathan Woetzel

Jeff does private deals between the West and the developing economies, mostly US-Asia and mostly healthcare. His background was shaped by eight years working for

Prince Alwaleed, nicknamed the "Prince of Deals" and the "Arabian Warren Buffett". Jeff lives in New York and Beijing and is a dedicated caffeine addict.

Jeffrey Towson

We are both micro analysts at heart, which means we like to stay in the business trenches. We focus almost entirely on individual companies and industries. And we both, more or less, avoid macro questions and analysis. Jonathan spends most of his time in CEOs' offices and boardrooms. Jeff spends most of his time looking at deals and advising healthcare companies. Jonathan is known for meeting with Fortune 500 CEOs in 2-3 different countries per week. Jeff is more known for picking fights with economists at China conferences.

Our academic home is Peking University's Guanghua School of Management in Beijing. It is in the epicenter of China business and is a great place to teach but the breathing masks do take some getting used to. We teach MBAs and Masters of Finance students from China and virtually the entire world. Our students are an absolute pleasure to work with.

An important note: Some of our students were involved in this book. We have highlighted them at the end of this chapter. If you are a CEO, managing director, HR head, executive recruiter or just curious, please take a look at these students.

THE ONLY FIVE STORIES YOU NEED TO KNOW TO UNDERSTAND THE FIGHT FOR CHINESE CONSUMERS

Consumers and competition are always intertwined. You can't understand one without the other. It's not just if people like mobile phones and if they can afford them. It's also what products companies like Apple, Samsung, and Xiaomi are offering and at what price. Consumer demands drive product development. But competitive dynamics also shape consumer behavior. If there is only one restaurant in the airport terminal, guess where all the customers go? In China, both of these factors can be particularly extreme. Consumers can be unpredictable and overwhelming, which can be great. But competition can be fast and ruthless, which can be brutal. And as mentioned in the Bobbie Bear story, you can also have the State as a major force, influencing and shaping competition on an ongoing basis.

So in this book we are going to tell you five stories, each of which details an important rising Chinese consumer demographic. And in each story we will also outline an important combination of customers, competition and government. If you can understand these five stories and the competitive situations they illustrate, you can understand much of what is going on with Chinese consumers today.

We have summarized these five situations in one graphic, called the China Consumer Pyramid (shown below). And that's our value proposition to you. You give us one hour (and four dollars) and we will give you five stories and one graphic that explain most of the fight for one billion Chinese consumers.

We will walk you through the graphic in each chapter. For those that are more interested in competitive strategy, there is additional discussion about our approach in the book's Appendix. Our one-sentence summary is that if Michael Porter says competition is about five forces and Warren Buffett says it is mostly about one (competitive advantage), we humbly suggest that competition in China is mostly about two factors: competitive advantage and the role of the State. And these are the factors that determine the two axes of our pyramid, as shown below in more detail.

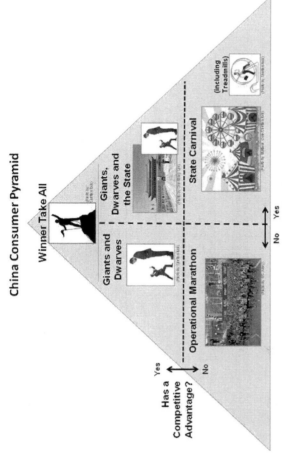

China Consumer Pyramid

Winner Take All

Giants, Dwarves and the State

Giants and Dwarves

State Carnival

(including Treadmills)

Operational Marathon

Has a Competitive Advantage?

Yes ← → No

Is the State an Active Force?

No ← → Yes

- Are strategic (not commercial) SOEs direct competitors?
- Are regulations against industry development or types of companies?
- Are regulations actively fueling the industry or types of companies?
- Are State-related assets or capabilities decisive in competition?

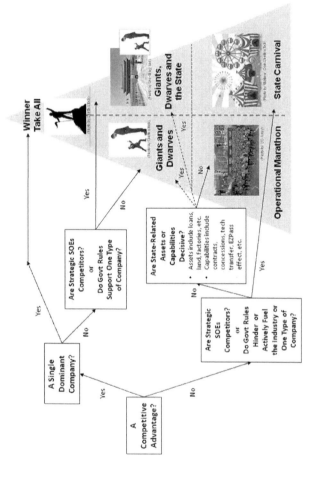

China Consumer Pyramid

A Competitive Advantage?

A Single Dominant Company?

Are Strategic SOEs Competitors? or Do Govt Rules Support One Type of Company?

Are State-Related Assets or Capabilities Decisive?
- Assets include loans, land, factories, etc.
- Capabilities include contracts, concessions, tech transfer, EZPass effect, etc.

Are Strategic SOEs Competitors? or Do Govt Rules Hinder or Actively Fuel the Industry or One Type of Company?

Winner Take All

Giants and Dwarves

Giants, Dwarves and the State

Operational Marathon

State Carnival

THIS IS AN INSPIRING STORY WITH SOME PRETTY GRUESOME FIGHTING MIXED IN

This book is a mix of two different views of China. One is a look at hundreds of millions of regular people moving into the middle class. The other is a look at the vicious fighting to capture them. One view is uplifting. The other is pretty gruesome entertainment.

Rising Chinese consumers are much debated and studied by businesses, governments and investors everywhere. They are the big new thing. But the irony is Chinese consumers are probably the oldest phenomenon in business history. Go back three hundred years and there was no United States. Much of what we now consider American business, economics and consumers did not exist. Go back three thousand years and there was similarly no England. Go back six thousand years and much of what we consider civilization and economics did not yet exist.

But at that time and ever since, there have been Chinese consumers. There have been millions of people buying food, clothes and homes in what is now called Beijing, Shanghai and Mainland China. It appears impossible to identify a time when civilization existed but Chinese consumers did not. Chinese consumers may well be the only truly permanent aspect of global business. So the idea that this is some new phenomenon is pretty ironic.

The real new phenomenon here is the fight for these consumers as they return to wealth. And it is difficult to accurately describe the viciousness of this fight. The daily competition between Chinese companies, Chinese State-owned enterprises (SOEs) and foreign companies for these rising consumers is absolutely brutal. And there are far more corpses than winners. It is arguably history's most well-funded knife fight.

Our position on all of this is simple (i.e., this is our three point summary for the entire book):

Point 1: China is now the world's most complicated consumer market.

It is big and growing fast. But it is also far more complex and dynamic than commonly believed. The complexity of Chinese consumers is increasing exponentially with wealth. You have to look at it sub-group by sub-group.

Point 2: The importance of China's rising consumers is matched only by the brutality of the fight for them.

The competition is utterly ruthless and most companies fail.

Point 3: The State ultimately creates most of the winners.

China is still State capitalism and, even in consumer markets, the government is still determining most of the winners.

Hopefully you will find the following five stories entertaining. They detail the successes and failures of Carlsberg, KFC, Christie's, the NBA and others in consumer China. And ultimately they tell the story of how Chinese consumers are finally becoming wealthy again – and how Western companies are finally learning to live with communism.

OUR THANKS FOR READING

We have tried to distill as much value as possible into a short and easily readable book. We hope you find it helpful or at least a good way to kill an hour.

We are posting videos and discussions for each of the chapters at www.onehourchina.com. The Appendix of this book also has a lot of additional material, particularly related to the impact of the State on competitive strategy. So there is lots more information if you would like to spend more than an hour.

Our thanks for reading and cheers,
Jonathan and Jeff
January 2015

Frustrated by long delivery times, Chinese car owners have been known to smash their cars in protest.
(photo by ImagineChina)

MBAS YOU SHOULD HAVE ON YOUR RADAR

Please take a quick look at the people who have worked on this book. They are awesome and should definitely be on your radar.

CHAPTER 1 ON KFC

FEDERICA BROCCHINI

Federica graduated from Bocconi University in Milan, Italy with a focus in finance. She also studied at the University of British Columbia in Vancouver and at Peking University in Beijing. She is currently working in investment banking in London.

AUDREY KHOO HUAI KUAN
Audrey is a Master's student at Humboldt-Universität zu Berlin. Fluent in English, Mandarin and German, she has deep expertise in European and Asian business.

FEDERICA LUSSANA
Federica graduated from Bocconi University in Milan, Italy with a Bachelor's degree in Economics and Business Administration. She is currently in her second year of a Master's of Science in Accounting, Finance, and Control. She also studied at Peking University and at the University of North Carolina, Kenan-Flagler Business School.

CHAPTER 2 ON CARLSBERG

PATRICK PFEIFFER
Patrick received a Master's of Science in Management from the European Business School in Germany. He completed exchange semesters at Peking University in China, as well as in Spain and the UK. Patrick has experience in private equity, investment banking, and asset management.

CHAPTER 3 ON CHRISTIE'S AND SOTHEBY'S

GRACEN DUFFIELD
Gracen holds an undergraduate degree from the University of Texas at Austin and a Master's in Business Administration from Peking University. An IT operations advisor

by background, she has a long-term interest in art and investing.

JEESAN HAN

Jeesan is an MBA candidate at the Peking University Guanghua School of Management. She previously completed a Bachelor's in Hospitality Administration at Boston University. Her area of expertise is real estate development, with a focus on hospitality and commercial properties. She is an Assistant Director at Kimreeaa Gallery in South Korea.

CHAPTER 4 ON FU SHOU YUAN

ALEXIA SHAO

Alexia was born and raised in France, with a combined French and Chinese upbringing. She holds a MSc. in Management from the ESSEC Business School-Grande Ecole program in Paris, where she specialized in Cultural Management and Art History with the Ecole du Louvre. She studied at Peking University and currently works as an analyst in Private Wealth Management at Goldman Sachs in Geneva.

CHAPTER 5 ON THE NBA

SHAN HAQUE

Shan is a Senior Associate at PricewaterhouseCoopers focused on automobiles and industrials. Previously, Shan co-founded the e-commerce platform Where's Mechanic, and consulted with investment management firms on operational best practices. Shan earned his MBA from the UCLA Anderson School of Management and his undergraduate degree in Finance from DePaul University.

NIALL SANTAMARIA

Niall focuses on international expansions and technology development in the TMT sector. Prior to starting his MBA at the London Business School, he worked in strategy consultancy and at Top Right Group, an international media group. He also works part-time with Exodus Ventures, analyzing business models for media and technology start-ups. He has studied at the China Europe International Business School in Shanghai. An avid sports fan, he has a keen interest in the English Premier League and in particular Liverpool FC.

CHETAK SHAH

Chetak earned an MBA from the Rotman School of Management in Toronto, Canada where he currently lives. He is pursuing a career in real estate investment.

***

We would also like to thank Daniel Singer of the Masters of Finance program at Peking University, Di Cai, Eric Almeraz, Wang Lihong, Jennifer Jin, Paul Gillis, Kai Lam, Heidi Austad Van Doren and Vagif Karimli. And a special thanks to Kendall Bitonte and Cleopatra Wise of Peking University. It has been a real pleasure working with you both on this project.

***

And finally, we would like to thank Glenn Leibowitz, who is Head of Marketing for One Hour China. He is the marketing guru who figured out how to put a speed-read China book on the best-seller list and keep it there. After a year, we are still in the top 10 for China on Amazon (and usually a couple spots ahead of Henry Kissinger).

CHAPTER #1:
HOW KFC BECAME CHINESE HEALTH FOOD

The following are some of China's food scandals. It's a long list but we encourage you to read them all.

Poisonous ham scandal (2003): Several small farmers were found to be producing hams outside of the normal season and then treating them with pesticides to keep them from spoiling. The main pesticide identified was Dichlorvos, an insecticide used in fumigation.

Fake baby formula scandal (2004): Approximately 140 Chinese factories were found to have produced fake milk powder that resulted in the deaths of at least 13 babies and made another 100-200 babies sick. It was named "big head disease" because after drinking the formula, the babies' heads would swell while their bodies became thinner from malnourishment.

Human hair soy sauce scandal (2004): An investigative report discovered soy sauce was being manufactured with an amino acid extraction process using hair collected from hair salons, barbershops and other locations.

School lunch poisoning scandal (2006): Three hundred students at an elementary school were poisoned by their school lunches. Two hundred students were hospitalized with headaches, fevers, vomiting and diarrhea.

Aluminium Chinese dumplings scandal (2008): After testing 700 samples of local foods containing flour, such as dumplings and steamed buns, Shenzhen health officials found that approximately one third contained aluminium.

Gutter oil scandal (2010): A report from a polytechnic university discovered that recycled oil was being used in at least one in 10 meals. The State Food and Drug Administration began a national investigation of so-called gutter oil.

Leather milk scandal (2011): Milk was discovered to have been manufactured using proteins left over from the process of leather softening at local tanneries.

Toxic bean sprout scandal (2011): Forty tons of bean sprouts treated with sodium nitrite, urea and antibiotics were found in Shenyang. The "poison bean sprouts" grew faster and looked "shinier" in market stalls.

Exploding watermelon scandal (2011): Melons that were treated with the chemical forchlorfenuron, which was supposed to boost growth, started blowing up. The melons split and sometimes literally exploded.

Exploding Chinese watermelons
(photo by ImagineChina)

Floating pig scandal (2013): Over 15,000 dead pigs floated down Shanghai's Huangpu River, the result of a crackdown on the illegal pig trade in upstream Zhejiang. Pork dealers had been buying diseased meat, processing it, and then reintroducing it into the market. They had dumped the pigs in the river to avoid the police.

Rat hot-pot scandal (2013): The Ministry of Public Security warned Shanghai consumers that some lamb meat being used in the city was in reality rat, mink, or fox. The substitute meat was mixed with gelatine, red pigment and nitrates to make it appear as lamb.

Waxy beef scandal (2013): Six workshops in Xi'an were discovered to be producing fake beef. They were accomplishing this by mixing pork meat with paraffin wax and industrial salts.

Melamine milk scandal (2008): Six babies died and approximately 290,000 became sick after drinking baby formula containing melamine. Melamine is high in nitrogen and adding it results in higher protein levels on tests.

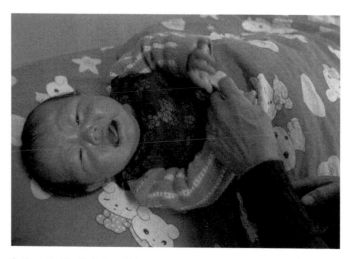

An 8 month old suffering from kidney stones caused by tainted milk powder. An estimated 290,000 babies were victims of the melamine milk scandal.
(photo by ImagineChina)

***

That was a long list for a self-proclaimed short book. But after reading the ninth or tenth story, the food safety issue really starts to hit home. Imagine hearing such stories year after year for most of your life. How comfortable would you be buying food in local restaurants or on the street? How about buying milk for your baby? The frequency of these scandals has made food safety a very deep part of Chinese consumer psychology.

This chapter is about **how food scandals have collided with China's rising consumers in a powerful way.** And what this means for leading restaurants like KFC.

Our starting point for this story is the rapidly rising and mostly urban middle class. This is arguably the most important consumer demographic in China today. We will make a few key points on this and then get to our story for this chapter.

KEY POINT 1: CHINA'S ONE BILLION CONSUMERS ARE FINALLY, AT LONG LAST, BUYING STUFF

In the past 25 years, disposable income per capita has increased by almost 500% in Chinese cities. That's just fantastic. And disposable income is really the number to watch here.

Since 1990, Chinese urban disposable income per capita has grown by 500%

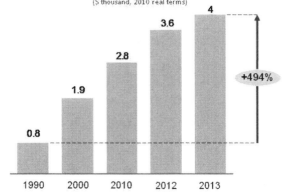

($ thousand, 2010 real terms)

Source: The World Bank, National Bureau of Statistics of China

However, here's the problem. Despite rising income and three decades of +10% GDP growth, spending by China's consumers just didn't happen. Spending growth has long lagged growth in GDP, exports and investment. And as recently as 2005, total consumer spending was still under $1T USD. Household wealth had definitely been accumulating but Chinese simply weren't spending.

In the last five years, this has finally, thankfully, started to change. By 2013, consumer spending had increased to $2.1T. And Chinese consumers replaced the Japanese as the second largest consumer group. And even at #2, they are still rocketing upwards. Chinese consumer spending is expected to reach $4-5T by 2020. Chinese consumers have finally arrived.

KEY POINT 2: CHINA'S RISING MIDDLE CLASS IS AN URBAN PHENOMENON

Most of this new spending is coming from the Chinese middle class, a group that really didn't exist 10 years ago. We define these middle class households as those with over $10,000 in annual income. This is much less than the $30,000 in the US but stuff is cheaper in China. These middle class households are the most important consumer demographic in China today. And they are overwhelmingly an urban phenomenon.

While the countryside did well in the early days of reform, the productivity gap with the cities has since widened dramatically. The productivity gap between the average city person and his/her rural counterpart is now around 300%. This reflects a whole bunch of factors that Jonathan would love to go into, but we will save them for the One Hour China Urbanization book (coming in late 2015). Basically, cities give you the market, skills and capital to achieve a middle class income. Not much of that happens in the countryside.

However, "urban" is not exactly the same thing as cities. Most income (and therefore consumer spending) will not be in big cities like Shanghai and Beijing. It will be in smaller Chinese cities, because there are a whole lot more of them. A city with 500,000 population is small by Chinese standards and there are about 600 of them. In the US, there are about 30.

But these are not really stand-alone small cities. They are typically linked to the big cities by physical, financial or administrative infrastructure. What we really have emerging in China today is rising middle class households living in linked "urban clusters". These urban clusters each have 30-80M people and 10-60 linked cities. And each cluster is about the size of a big European country. What we are seeing today is a surge in urban income and spending across a huge number of smaller cities, linked-up in clusters.

Chinese middle class households are a "linked-city", urban phenomenon.
(photo by Kzenon/Shutterstock)

KEY POINT 3: "MAINSTREAM CONSUMERS" ARE THE CRITICAL NEW DEMOGRAPHIC

Chinese middle class households are urban and rising. And by most estimates, their incomes will double from 2010 to 2020, reaching about $8,000 per capita. They will then be similar to South Korea and other Asian countries, but still way below the United States ($35,000) and Japan ($25,000). Chinese consumers are going to be far more numerous but also nominally poorer than those of developed countries (yet also wealthier than other developing countries.)

As this increase in income happens, an important change is occurring. A new group is emerging which McKinsey has labeled the new "mainstream consumers". As shown below, new this group, which has household incomes of $16,000 to $34,000, was 6% of urban households in 2010. But by 2020, they will be 51% – an annual growth rate of approximately 26%. The emergence of new mainstream consumers is causing an important shift in spending and behavior.

New mainstream consumers will be >50% of Chinese households by 2020

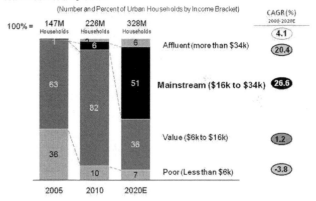

Source: McKinsey Insights China – Macroeconomic model update

To date, much of the China consumer story has been about "value" consumers. These are consumers with household incomes between $6,000 and $16,000 per year. And they tend to care most about getting good value for their money. They want a low price. They want acceptable quality. And they are pragmatic, as opposed to emotional. As the new mainstream group emerges, this value group is going to decrease from 82% of urban households in 2010 to only 7% by 2020.

The distinction between value and mainstream is important. What is really happening is a big upgrade in lifestyles and a shift of priorities. They are shifting from buying the basic necessities of life, such as housing, food and healthcare, to more discretionary purchases, such as cars, overseas trips and lattes. This new mainstream population can afford homes, cars and some small luxury items. They care about quality and experience, not just price. They save less and are willing to pay brand premiums. They also shop online a lot. By 2020, the number of mainstream consumers will be 400M, comprising about 167M households.

Given this bifurcation in the market between value and new mainstream consumers, winning companies usually need a ladder of price points, reflecting the different habits of the two segments. For example, in toothpaste, Procter & Gamble focuses on the need for whitening in the high end where they can charge a premium. A lot of this is accomplished through better packaging and merchandising. Meanwhile, they simultaneously offer more basic SKUs at a 40% discount to premium, in order to be competitive with the value consumers.

***

Okay, that was a bit of theory. Let's get to our first story. And it is a story about what happens when these rising urban Chinese middle class consumers decide they care deeply about something, like food safety.

THE AWESOME STORY OF SAMUEL SU AND KFC CHINA

KFC China began in 1987 and today has over 4,500 restaurants. They are the number one quick-service chain in the Mainland and are, without question, the most successful restaurant company in China. This is a well-known story and we are not going to repeat it here. Our focus is on how KFC's awesome China success can mostly be attributed to the business acumen of one man, Samuel Su.

Sam Su was born and raised in Taiwan. He attended National Taiwan University and graduated with a degree in chemical engineering. He eventually migrated to business, got an MBA from Wharton and was working as a marketing manager at Proctor & Gamble (Germany and Taiwan) when KFC came calling.

Sam joined KFC under unusual circumstances. While they had opened in China in 1987, they had only four China restaurants when Sam joined in 1989. And KFC at that time was owned by PepsiCo, a highly decentralized company with expertise mostly in beverages, not restaurants. So KFC was a restaurant company with a minimal

China presence and no real restaurant expertise at the top. That made it very different from global leader McDonald's, which had restaurant managers at the helm and highly centralized international controls.

KFC opened its first China restaurant in Beijing in 1987. It averaged 9,000 customers per day and reportedly made back its investment in one year. KFC's initial China splash was not surprising. There was a lot of excitement around Western products at that time. The food was different. And the restaurants were clean and professionally run. It was all very interesting in China in 1987. The wide-scale advertising probably also helped. So likely did the air conditioning.

Sam became Regional Marketing Manager for North Asia and also acting General Manager for the four KFC restaurants in China. He hired additional managers (mostly from Taiwan) and promptly went on a restaurant-opening binge. Jonathan became a KFC China fan in the 1980's because of their outlet on the Shanghai Bund. That outlet has since become the Waldorf Astoria Shanghai. So you get a sense of how good Sam was at getting great locations.

KFC's current owner, Yum! Brands (spun out from PepsiCo), is known for being particularly effective at international franchising. But back in China in the 1990's, Sam had to operate mostly through joint ventures by law. That gave him a greater degree of control and increased equity, but also made opening restaurants slower and a lot more expensive. Sam turned out to be a unique manager in a unique situation. Because of PepsiCo's decentralized approach, he was able to operate very independently in China, opening stores rapidly and customizing the menus to the point they were almost unrecognizable to KFC in the USA. But at the same time, he was also very well-funded from headquarters and able to spend aggressively on growth, which was expensive. This decentralized, independent but well-funded approach turned out to be the right strategy for China. By 1994, Sam had 28 KFC restaurants in China. By 1997, he had 100. He was also put in charge of Pizza Hut China during this period.

But KFC in China was not a story of explosive growth. Compared to many China businesses launched in the 1990's, restaurants actually grew quite slowly. By 1997, market leader KFC had only 100 outlets. And second-place McDonald's had only 29 restaurants in Beijing. Given the population of China, both companies could probably have opened thousands of outlets.

Compare restaurants to other China businesses. Real estate developer China Vanke went from its first residential project in 1988 to building 50,000-80,000 apartments per year. Instant noodle company Tingyi went from a Mainland start-up in 1992 to a +$15B company today. The story of restaurants for 1990-2010 is really one of slow steady building – not explosive growth. KFC entered earlier than most and built their business steadily and consistently over decades. Sam spent a lot of time and money building supporting operations (food sourcing, warehousing, logistics, employee recruiting and training, etc.). He opened stores city by city and region by region.

He eventually reached 4,500 KFCs, double what McDonald's has, but it took over 20 years of work.

Yum! Brands has, to their credit, recognized Sam and promoted him over and over again to the point where he now reports to the Chairman directly. He is CEO and Chairman of Yum! Restaurants China and also Vice Chairman of the Board for Yum! Brands. Sam oversees over 6,200 restaurants in China in more than 900 cities. This includes 4,500 KFC restaurants, 1,000 Pizza Hut restaurants and approximately 200 Pizza Hut Home Service units. Yum! typically opens at least 700 new restaurants in China per year, about 2 outlets per day.

Samuel Su, China's most successful restaurant manager
(photo by ImagineChina)

HOW KFC BECAME HEALTH FOOD IN CHINA

That brings us back to the discussed food scandals. As shown in the below chart, food safety is one of the top 5-6 concerns of Chinese residents nationally, above even unemployment and crime. And according to a poll taken after the 2010 earthquake in Qinghai, Chinese consumers rate food safety as their second highest concern after earthquakes – and ahead of cancer, unsafe water and drunk driving.

Top concerns of Chinese residents (2013)

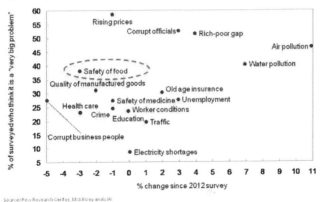

Source: Pew Research Center, McKinsey analysis

And this is not going away any time soon in China. The domestic food supply chain is highly fragmented and bad products can easily be introduced by bad actors almost anywhere along it. According to Mintel Group, there are approximately 500,000 food production and processing companies in China. And approximately 70% of them have under 10 employees. How do you ensure the quality of a food chain that mostly looks like the below picture?

Domestic farms remain underdeveloped
(photo by Giancarlo Liguori/Shutterstock)

In the last two years, food scandals have really hit the media in China. And this has caused a lot of pain for restaurants. Sales have fallen across the industry and at KFC. But we argue that what is really happening is a painful but necessary transition process. The risk of a food scandal is forcing everyone to change their businesses – to protect their brands, to improve their quality controls, to train their management and to build new operations. Those that respond the best to this challenge will have their reputations enhanced and their businesses strengthened, relative to most competitors. This is our contrarian argument – that food scandals are helping certain restaurants like KFC and McDonalds in China.

In 2013, some of our students surveyed +100 Beijing residents about their eating habits. When asked to describe McDonald's, there was a surprising result. The most common words chosen were "time-saving" and "safety". Participants strongly associated McDonald's not just with being Western quick service (i.e., fast food), but also with being clean and safe. The survey also found that 70% believed that McDonald's food is generally healthy, as opposed to just safe. The company was overwhelmingly regarded as offering safe, fast and healthy food. It turns out health food in China is less about salt and fat, and more about the absence of toxic chemicals.

Through advertising campaigns and other initiatives, you can see leading companies like KFC and McDonald's reinforcing their reputations as restaurants you can trust. McDonald's advertisements show fresh vegetables and produce. Cleanliness and hygiene are now a big part of branding in the food business in China.

But it's not just about having a Western brand and clean food. It's also the clean dining areas. It's the professionally trained staff. It's the customers' beliefs about the ingredients going into the food. For example, McDonald's offers its customers short tours of its kitchens so you can see how clean they are. You can see where the employees wash their hands and how the food is handled. On KFC's and McDonald's China websites, you can find sections on kitchen sanitation and hygiene practices. You can find details on how often kitchen employees are required to wash their hands, and that the procedure should last at least 20 seconds. You can find out how different color gloves are used for cooked and uncooked food. After reading the scandals at the beginning of this chapter, you can see how such initiatives really do make an impression.

However, if you are operating in the food industry in China, you are going to have a food safety issue at some point. It is inevitable. And if there isn't a real issue, then one will likely be manufactured by a competitor or the media (especially if you are foreign and well-known). So it is also important to be able to play defense.

In 2014, a Chinese State television report accused OSI, a major supplier to the Chinese operations of KFC, Pizza Hut, and Starbucks, of processing expired beef and chicken products. In terms of China food scandals, this was negligible. Nobody got sick and such things happen at virtually every restaurant in China. But because it was about foreign companies it was widely reported in the media.

While most local companies react to such situations by being evasive or generally disorganized, Yum! issued an apology about an hour after the report aired. In addition, within three days they required all China KFC and Pizza Hut restaurants to stop using all meat supplied by the factory. Moreover, they cut ties with OSI globally, including in Australia and the United States. Not only was this effective "fast defense" to the situation, but the speed also made it smart offense. The transparency and swiftness of the response actually reinforced their image as a responsible and safe company.

You can see there are multiple factors playing out here. Rising urban consumers, food safety issues transforming the industry, restaurants competing and how management responds. And per our thesis, these situations are overwhelmingly determined by three factors: consumers, competition and government. In this case, we call the combination of these factors an Operational Marathon.

***

KEY POINT 4: RESTAURANTS IN CHINA ARE AN OPERATIONAL MARATHON

While urban middle class consumers wanting a safe lunch are an attractive demographic, the competitive situation in Chinese restaurants is unfortunately very difficult. The industry is overwhelmingly shaped by the particularly intense local competition. We call this difficult situation an Operational Marathon.

In an Operational Marathon, you do not have a competitive advantage or any real barrier to entry against competitors. You don't have any unique technologies, special government permits or obviously powerful economics (customer capture, production advantages, economies of scale, etc.). So you are not competing against 3-4 companies. You are competing against hundreds and really thousands of existing and potential competitors. And in China, that should give you pause. Because this is a huge country with a lot of really hard-working people. While many competitors will be small and amateurish, others will be professional and very well-funded. And everyone will work really, really hard. The Chinese restaurant business is basically a never-ending marathon against a sea of other runners (basically the picture shown below).

Restaurants in China are an Operational Marathon.
(photo by David P Lewis / Shutterstock)

We have named this situation Operational Marathon because to win (a relative term here), you need to constantly improve your operating efficiencies and increase your operating scale. You must grow restaurant by restaurant. You must build your supply chain. You must train management. You must build warehouses and cut your logistics costs. In order to survive, you are constantly struggling to increase your productivity and size, relative to a sea of competitors. And you advertise, advertise, advertise.

And like a marathon, this race goes on for a very long time. You are basically doing the same activities as all your competitors. You are just trying to do them a little bit faster and better. And you hope that over years you slowly pull out from the pack and eventually get so far ahead that you are difficult to catch. But the race never really ends. You are never really protected from your competition (i.e., no competitive advantage). Even after twenty years of effective management, one stumble and fall (say in a food scandal) and they can all catch up.

In Operational Marathons, there is no competitive advantage and the State is not an active force, except for typical regulations. This puts them in the bottom left of our pyramid. This is a very big category with tons of companies. It is the most common situation in China (hence the wider base of the pyramid). And life at the bottom of the pyramid in China is not easy. In fact, it is usually ruthlessly competitive and pretty Darwinian. Most of the China horror stories you hear are this situation.

For those who are interested in how we define these situations more specifically, please refer to the flow chart below. Otherwise, you can just skip it.

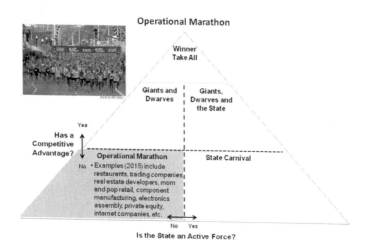

Operational Marathon

Winner Take All

| Giants and Dwarves | Giants, Dwarves and the State |

Operational Marathon
- Examples (2015) include restaurants, trading companies, real estate developers, mom and pop retail, component manufacturing, electronics assembly, private equity, internet companies, etc.

State Carnival

Has a Competitive Advantage? — Yes / No

Is the State an Active Force? — No / Yes

Operational Marathon

A Competitive Advantage?
No →

Are Strategic SOEs Competitors? or **Do Govt Rules Hinder or Actively Fuel the Industry or One Type of Company?**
No →

Are State-Related Assets or Capabilities Decisive?
- Assets include loans, land, factories, etc.
- Capabilities include contracts, concessions, tech transfer, EZPass effect, etc.
No →

Operational Marathon
→
- No barriers to entry or competitive advantages.
- No significant role of State – an even, economic and difficult playing field.
- Mgmt performance critical. Speed & early entry helps.
- Focus on operational efficiencies & operational scale.

Consider how much competition KFC actually faces in China. There are full-service Chinese restaurants, foreign quick-serve restaurants, local chains and even food carts. In 2009, there were about 2.8M independent full-service restaurants alone (that's the huge crowd running next to you). And despite +6,000 years of Chinese restaurant history, no restaurant chain has even 1-2% marketshare. That factoid should give you a sense of how difficult this industry is.

In this situation, steady and consistent progress, not explosive growth, is actually exactly what you would hope to see. And that is really what we have seen from KFC. From day one, they have faced a huge number of competitors in a highly fragmented market. But they ran hard and made no major mistakes. They steadily increased their operational scale and operating efficiencies – and over time they have slowly pulled away from the pack.

And here we have one of the quirks that makes business in China so much fun. Because increasing concerns about food safety are creating the possibility of having a competitive advantage in restaurants for the first time.

By and large, restaurants are not known for having particularly powerful competitive advantages. You can gain some scale in advertising. Good real estate locations and branding help as well. But if you are in an industry with food safety issues, this creates big new operating requirements. You have to ensure quality from farm to table. You need to manage the warehouses, the trucks and even the farms. That is operationally difficult and creates big fixed costs. So these food safety issues are creating large fixed costs that most local restaurants simply cannot afford. It is giving the leaders like KFC the opportunity to expand their quality-safety proposition beyond just clean kitchens.

China's restaurant industry has weathered some difficult years. But leading companies like KFC are now coming out of it smarter, with enhanced reputations for quality and with the opportunity to develop real competitive advantages around the increased operational requirements of food safety. Food safety may be creating an important change from a traditional Operational Marathon.

And that brings us back to Sam Su. For most of the past two decades, KFC has been in an Operational Marathon in China. They had no real competitive advantage. And while they had strengths (brand, expertise, cash, management, etc.), they succeeded mostly by being smart and building their business step by step over a long, long time. Superior managers like Sam were critical. Now KFC is way out in front of the pack and accelerating on the rising spending of middle class urban consumers. It is now their race to lose.

FINAL POINT: RESTAURANTS IN CHINA ARE A VERY DIFFICULT BUSINESS

Think of all the challenges you would face as a manager of a China restaurant business. Are you getting the best locations for the stores (location, location, location)? Are you recruiting and training enough staff (McDonald's has >60,000 China employees)? Are you actively marketing to both value and mainstream urban Chinese? Can you actually make a good burger or chicken breast for under $5 in 5 minutes? And can you do it consistently thousands of times per day? Are you localizing your products for Chinese tastes (is rice on the menu)? Can you manage a supply chain of thousands of food products from around China given pervasive quality problems? Oh and by the way, market leader KFC opens 1-2 new restaurants every day in China. How many are you opening this week?

Restaurants are tough, operational, local service businesses with no real protection. It's a ruthless space and Chinese restaurants have been competing with each other forever. The world's oldest restaurant is actually in China. It is called Ma Yu Ching's Bucket Chicken House and has been in business since AD 1153.

Jeff has long argued to our students that you don't go to Kenya to compete in long-distance running and you don't go to China to compete in restaurants. Chinese restaurants (and the Kenyans) will run you into the ground. KFC became the leader in China largely because very effective managers like Sam Su worked very hard for decades. It also has to do with the fact that Chinese consumers really like chicken.

KFC has had exceptionally smart China management. However, saying they are smart (which they are) sounds like a compliment (which it is). But in another sense it is also a red flag. Warren Buffett has famously said that he likes businesses that are so wonderful that an idiot can run them, because "sooner or later, one will". His point is, you don't necessarily want the success of your business to require really smart management every day. That's very hard and pretty rare. The best China consumer businesses are those where you only have to be smart one time – and then you can just relax. More on that situation in the next chapter.

Zhangjiajie in Hunan (of Avatar fame) is arguably China's best tourist site. The top of the mountain also has only one restaurant, an unbelievably large two-story McDonald's. A tip of the hat to whoever did that deal. Impressive.
(photo by Ayolography / Shutterstock)

CHAPTER #2:
HOW CARLSBERG BEER CRASHED THE CHINA PARTY

Question #1: **What is the world's most popular beer?**

(Write it down or pick an answer in your head).

Question #2: **How many of the world's top 10 beers are Chinese?**

(Again, don't go on until you have an answer).

We might be the first authors to try to give a pop quiz in a book. But we are professors and pop quizzes are one of the few perks of the job (excessive facial hair is another). Anyways, the answers are "Snow" and "three".

Yes, the world's top beer by volume is Snow. If you haven't heard of it, don't worry. It really isn't drunk anywhere outside China. If you try it, prepare to be underwhelmed. The top 10 beers by volume in 2013 were (in order) Snow, Tsingtao, Bud Light, Budweiser, Skol, Yanjing, Heineken, Harbin, Brahma and Coors Light. Three are Chinese (Snow, Tsingtao and Yanjing).

The point is that beer is very popular with Chinese consumers – and has been for a long time.

**

There are reports of beer in China as far back as 5000 BC. And there is pretty good evidence it was being drunk regularly by 23 BC, when it was known as "kiu". But we will begin our story with China's first modern brewery, which was built in 1900. That first brewery was established by a German-Polish immigrant in the Northern city of Harbin and was mostly for Russians working on the Trans-Manchurian railway. Other breweries were set up around the same time by Russians, Germans and even Czechs. But it was the Anglo-German Brewery Co. founded by German and British merchants in Qingdao in 1903 that would become the most famous. That brewery evolved into Tsingtao, currently number 2 on the top 10 list.

However, it was actually the Communist Party that turned China into a uniformly beer-drinking country. After the founding of the People's Republic of China in 1949, investments in beer increased dramatically and State-run breweries were built in most major cities, typically with 17,000 hectoliters of capacity each. This took China's total beer production from about 58,000 hectoliters per year in 1949 to over 3.3M hectoliters by the 1970's. More than 90 brewers eventually covered every province, city and autonomous region (except Tibet and Qinghai). These State-run breweries became the backbone of China's beer industry and are still a significant part of the industry's dynamics today.

This chapter is the story of **how one foreign beer maker, Carlsberg, beat the odds and succeeded in the China market.** And interestingly, their success had a lot to do with a new group of consumers emerging from China's vast Western interior.

KEY POINT 1: INLAND URBANITES ARE CHINA'S NEW CONSUMER FRONTIER

Inland China is the Western 50% of the country that, up until recently, nobody really talked about. If you combine Central and Western China, you have a truly massive geography that stretches from Henan to Xinjiang. It contains everything from major cities and manufacturing hubs to vast agricultural expanses, deserts and mountain towns. It is China's "big backyard".

China's "big backyard"

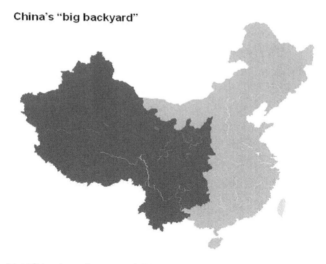

Inland China, depending on your definition, is about 50% of the country by geography – but not yet by people or money.

Western China (part of Inland China) is home to over 200M emerging middle class consumers. They are a critical new group of Chinese consumers and they are rising much faster than their coastal equivalents. Unsurprisingly, they also have much lower incomes. The average urban employed wages in Inland Yunnan and Gansu in 2013 were $3,410 and $3,400, compared with $6,980 in Beijing and $5,230 in Zhejiang (National Bureau of Statistics of China). And while coastal provinces like Guangdong and Zhejiang are about 65% urbanized, only 39% of the populations of Yunnan and Gansu live in cities. More agriculture and less urbanization generally means less money. So these Inland consumers are lower income but their incomes are growing significantly faster. Inland China was 13% of middle class consumers in 2002. By 2022, it will be 39%.

Inland China includes Chongqing, possibly the world's largest city.
(photo by JingAiping / Shutterstock)

Inland China also includes places like Yunnan…
(photo by gringos4 / Shutterstock)

...and even far-West places like Tibet.
(photo by Lian Deng / Shutterstock)

KEY POINT 2: INLAND CONSUMERS ARE STILL MOSTLY VALUE-FOCUSED

In Chapter 1, we wrote about the new mainstream consumers who are quickly becoming the majority in cities. And they are largely replacing the value-focused consumers that have been the majority for the past 15-20 years.

However, in the Inland regions, value consumers still dominate and are likely to continue to do so. They have significantly lower incomes and are very pragmatic. They mostly want functionality and a good price. On a monthly basis, they mostly worry about getting by. They typically have never driven a car. Most have never had a passport. And, unsurprisingly, they save as much as possible. Shopping is not entertainment. Every RMB counts.

Inland consumers are also generally not as experienced when it comes to things like technology, fashion and brands. Buying quality means a lot of experimentation to find out what works in their budgets. Typically, their most trusted way to learn about products is friends. And as they are less web-savvy than their coastal cousins, direct sales models tend to work better. Unsurprisingly, local marketers focus more on product girls in nightclubs and elaborate in-store displays.

KEY POINT 3: THE BIGGEST DIFFERENCES INLAND ARE ACTUALLY ON THE SUPPLY SIDE

Inland consumers are harder and more expensive to reach. Logistics costs in China can be above 15% of GDP, compared to less than 10% in the US. This problem gets much worse as you go West. The topography is also a problem. Some areas, like Southwestern China, are literally land-locked behind mountains. In Guizhou, it is said "you can't go three days without rain, three miles without mountains, or find three peasants with more than three RMB."

As you move West, the city clusters become less developed. The geographic distances become huge and there is less and less infrastructure. Inland road density is about 50% of what it is in the East. Plus, in many places, the roads have simply not been built yet. There aren't that many brands out West today and people are hungry for more products and services.

Western Xinjiang. Logistics are a major problem in Inland China.
(photo by Lian Deng / Shutterstock)

Companies that require national distribution are struggling to cover this vast territory. The recent IPOs of e-commerce giants Alibaba and JD.com both had fascinating details on their attempts to extend their logistics and distribution Inland. For instance, JD.com's fulfillment center in Xi'an serves Qinghai, Xinjiang and Ningxia. So, in theory, their couriers travel over 500 miles to reach Qinghai's capital. And their deliveries to Urumqi appear to involve a +1,500-mile journey.

The companies that are successful in supplying the West tend to be granular in their approach to different cities and regions. They create local armies on the ground in each region. For example, Tingyi, the multibillion-dollar Taiwanese noodle maker, divides the country into +15 territories, each with its own products, sales and distribution setups.

THE STORY OF SUNNY WONG AND CARLSBERG CHINA

Okay, back to Chinese beer and our story for this chapter.

This story starts in 1999 and it centers around a Hong Kong native and long-time Carlsberg employee named Sunny Wong. Sunny joined Carlsberg as a sales manager in Hong Kong in 1987. He rose through the ranks and eventually became General Manager for North China.

As he recounted in his TEDx Talk, he was 45 years old in 1999. He had a good life and a stable job with Carlsberg, a company he had worked at for 12 years. His wife had recently quit her job so she could spend time with their daughter, who was then in high school in the UK. And then one day in 1999, his boss came in to tell him that the company was basically leaving China – and that he was probably out of a job. This would turn out to be a pivotal moment for both him and Carlsberg.

To appreciate what a radical move this was for Carlsberg, consider the following factoids on beer in China today:

- China leads the world in total beer consumption. According to Euromonitor International, Chinese consumers drink about 520M hectoliters a year, roughly twice as much as Americans in the aggregate. But this is still much less on a per capita basis – 38 liters in China vs. 74 liters in the US (and 109 liters in Germany) in 2012. So this market is big and likely going to grow a lot.

- Beer is purchased regularly by Chinese of all income levels. Few companies can talk about going after one billion Chinese customers. Brewers can.

- From 2007 to 2012, the annual growth in Chinese beer drinking nationwide was 5.7%.

- 80-85% of lager currently sold in China is economy priced (about $1.20 per liter). This is a legacy of State-run breweries offering cheap beer for decades. "Premiumization" is a big topic and source of hope in Chinese beer circles.

- Finally, it is rumored (i.e., we have heard it but can't verify it) that you are more likely to find a beer in a Chinese refrigerator than in a refrigerator anywhere else in the world.

Per-capita beer consumption in China is growing steadily

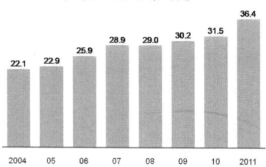

(Per Capita Chinese Beer Consumption (liters))

Source: Access Asia, Kirin Institute of Food and Lifestyle Report Vol. 22 (2003 Beer Consumption in Major Countries), Accenture analysis, China Economic Information Network

Basically, beer in China is **universally drunk, branded, and cheap.**

POST-OPENING, BEER PRODUCTION IN CHINA SURGED – AND INTERNATIONAL BREWERS GOT HAMMERED

A bit more history. With the opening of China in 1979, the beer industry exploded. Between 1979 and 1988, there was a 10-fold increase in the number of brewers in operation, reaching approximately 800. And total beer production increased 15-fold. China rocketed from 26th in the world in beer production to third, just behind Germany and the United States. And by 1993, China reached second in production with total output at 102M hecto-liters.

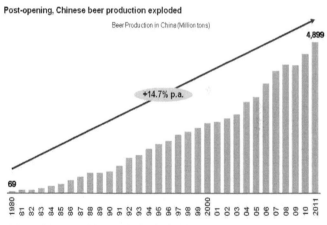

Post-opening, Chinese beer production exploded

Beer Production in China (Million tons)

4,899

+14.7% p.a.

69

1980 81 82 83 84 85 86 87 88 89 90 91 92 93 94 95 96 97 98 99 2000 01 02 03 04 05 06 07 08 09 10 2011

Source: China Industrial Economic Statistical Yearbook, data of 2010 from China National Sugar and Alcoholic commodities fak, EPS

This Chinese beer explosion did not go unnoticed by the big international brewers. Brewers such as Anheuser-Busch and Interbrew were some of the first foreign companies in China. They initially used agents to import and distribute their products, usually priced toward the higher end. Then they went hunting for breweries and deals. For example, Anheuser-Busch bought 4.5% of Tsingtao in 1993 for a mere $16M. They invested another $182M in October 2002 for a 22.4% stake. Most of the deal activity during this period was on attempted acquisitions of breweries.

Overall, things did not go terribly well for the international brewers. Low pricing made mainstream beer fairly unprofitable. And the Chinese State-owned enterprises (SOEs) ran the field, rapidly growing in size and taking market share region by region. After many difficult years, most of the international brewers withdrew, stuck with importing, or switched to one of the following three approaches.

APPROACH 1: STAY IN THE HIGH END.

This was Heineken's strategy. They shifted to a premium niche. This had a lot to do with the low pricing and profitability of mainstream Chinese beer. The average price of beer in China in 2012 was just $1.20 per liter, compared to $3.70 in the US and over $5 in Japan. China is currently #1 in volume but #8 in operating profits.

In 2012, Heineken acquired Asia Pacific Breweries (Tiger brand) in Singapore, and this increased their market share in premium lager in Southeast Asia and China. This placed them behind Anheuser-Busch InBev (AB-InBev) and ahead of Tsingtao in the premium market.

So far this strategy appears to have worked. Heineken is now one of the leading premium brands in China and has experienced double-digit growth in the premium segment in the last couple of years.

APPROACH 2: BECOME A GIANT (AND WAIT OUT THE LOW PRICING).

This is the China dream. To be a beer giant in the world's biggest beer market. But only one foreign beer maker has achieved it. And it was somewhat by accident. When InBev merged with Anheuser-Busch in 2008, this had an important effect on both companies' China businesses. The merged AB-InBev became the first and only foreign brewer among the top five in China.

InBev (previously Interbrew) had been active in China since 1984, but had struggled like the rest. Anheuser-Busch had done better and their Budweiser brand was a leading premium beer in China in terms of volume. Plus, they had their investment in Tsingtao. But as a merged entity, both companies jumped into the top tier. The Budweiser brand currently holds a 1.7% market share across all segments. Their mainstream brands include Budweiser, Harbin and Sedrin.

APPROACH 3: PARTNER WITH A MAJOR CHINESE SOE.

This is the "if you can't beat them, join them" variation of Approach 2. In 1994, global beer giant SABMiller created a joint venture (JV) with the State-owned China

Resources Enterprise called CR Snow. As mentioned in the pop quiz, Snow is now the most popular beer in the world. SABMiller has 49% of this JV.

CR Snow is now expanding its China market share, most recently from 15% in 2007 to 22% in 2012. CR Snow now operates more than 90 breweries across the country. They have over 30 local brands and continue to make acquisitions, such as Jiangsu Santai, Henan Blue and Kingway Brewery. And most importantly, by virtue of their partnership with China Resources they can reach 2.5M retail outlets in China. This will be an important factor going forward.

***

These have been the three main approaches by foreign brewers in China thus far. Go premium or go big if you can. Those who couldn't have struggled, failed or exited. Which brings us back to Carlsberg and Sunny Wong.

SUNNY AND CARLSBERG LEAVE CHINA

As mentioned, Sunny joined Carlsberg China as a sales manager in 1987, six years after Carlsberg had opened its first China brewery (in Hong Kong). Carlsberg's first big move on the Mainland came in 1995 when it acquired a brewery in Huizhou, Guangdong. They shifted all production from Hong Kong to this facility. They also purchased part of a brewery in Shanghai during this period.

But Carlsberg, like virtually every other foreign beer maker, struggled in China. Despite the attractive demographics, beer prices in China were low. And foreign companies found themselves at a disadvantage in terms of growth, both organic and by acquisition. The three giant brewers that emerged during this period, Yanjing, Tsingtao and China Resources, were all State-owned. And right behind them were Zhujiang and Kingstar, also State-owned.

Over time, regional markets had become increasingly dominated by certain beer companies. Tsingtao beer was strongest in East China. China Resources and Harbin were strong in the Northeast. And Yanjing beer was strong in the North. The market also developed a significant oversupply of production capacity – some argue as high as 40%. This, unsurprisingly, led to price wars and thus even smaller profit margins.

This came to a head in 1999 when Carlsberg appears to have decided to exit China. We don't know exactly what was going on internally. But by 1999, Carlsberg's competitors were starting to look much larger than them. In 2000, Carlsberg sold 75% of its Shanghai brewery to Tsingtao, with the remainder to be sold later. They also exited a 50/50 joint venture they had formed with the Thai company Chang Beverages Pte., Ltd. And in 1999, Sunny exited Carlsberg after 12 years and moved to the UK (where he enrolled in an MBA program).

SUNNY AND CARLSBERG PIONEER A GO WEST STRATEGY

What happened between 1999 and 2002 with Carlsberg is unclear to us as outsiders. What we do know is that beginning in 2002, Carlsberg began making a series of bold and surprising moves in China.

But they didn't partner with an SOE like SABMiller. Nor was there a merger like AB-InBev. And they didn't go premium like Heineken. Instead, they chose to leave the major China markets and go West, deep into Inland China. They exited Shanghai and Beijing and headed to Xinjiang and Yunnan. And in 2002, Sunny came back to Carlsberg and accepted what he has referred to as a "mission impossible task" - to go to West China and develop Carlsberg's business. He has joked that this was his first time to actually go to those places.

It was a daring strategy. Inland China was the one region that was not yet dominated by the large SOE brewers. It was still open territory. But you also need to have a picture in your mind of Western China circa 2003. It was the poorest part of China. It was a massive and undeveloped territory. There was little infrastructure and even less money. It was not the end of the earth, but you could probably see it from there.

Gansu province, one of Carlsberg's new core China markets
(photo by Rat007 / Shutterstock)

A review of Sunny's Carlsberg presentation in 2006 is fascinating. Western China had exceptionally low per-capita beer consumption. In Eastern China in 2005, it ranged from 30-80 liters per person, but in Tibet and Ningxia it was only 10-15 liters. And in Yunnan and Xinjiang it was closer to 3 liters. That could of course mean big growth one day. More likely, it meant small money in difficult geographies for the foreseeable future.

Carlsberg's "Go West" strategy hinged on acquisitions - basically a race for local scale. And they went on an impressive deal spree starting in 2003. Sunny was first sent to Yunnan. There Carlsberg acquired 100% of Kunming Huashi Brewery and Dali Beer Group. This was followed by the acquisition of the majority (first 33%, later increased to 50%) of Lhasa Brewery in Tibet. Then a majority share (30% later increased to 50%) in Lanzhou Huanghe's three breweries in the Gansu Province. Then an investment in a Greenfield brewery in Qinghai – with production starting in 2005 – and the acquisition of 34.5% of Wusu Brewery in Xinjiang Autonomous Region. In 2005, they increased their share in Wusu Brewery Group to 50%. And in 2006, through a joint venture with Ningxia Nongken Enterprise Group, they established a Greenfield brewery in Ningxia Autonomous Region. Carlsberg had 70% of that joint venture.

By 2006, Carlsberg had 20 breweries that covered half of the geography of China. And they were the market leader in all the Western provinces in which they had invested.

Carlsberg's Go West strategy really hinged on four factors:

First, they entered through JVs with local breweries. These breweries were the remnants of the discussed State-owned system, built over 40 years. Such SOE partnerships neutralize to some degree the disadvantages private companies (foreign and local) have when competing with SOE brewers.

Second, they built out local distribution in a vast and difficult part of China. The majority of sales were through wholesalers, which means locking up the best wholesalers and delivering beer to lots of little stores across a massive geography. To get the best wholesalers you have to have significant market share. And vice versa.

Carlsberg China in 2006

Lanzhou group
•3 breweries
•Market leader
•Brands: Huanghe

Ningxia group
•2 breweries
•Market leader
•Brands: Xixia beer

Xinjiang Wusu Beer group
•10 breweries
•Market leader
•Brands: Wusu, Xinjiang

Lhasa Brewery
•1 brewery
•Brands: Lhasa

Qinghai Huang He Brewery
•1 breweries
•Market leader
•Brands: Huanghe

Yunnan group
•2 breweries
•Market leader
•Brands: Dali, Windflower
Snow and Moon

Guangdong
•1 brewery

Xinjiang / Gansu / Qinghai / Tibet / Yunnan

Source: Data from Carlsberg China presentation, annual reports

Third, their products covered the whole customer range. Carlsberg's beer was priced to discount, mainstream, premium and super-premium. And this today includes Carlsberg Green Label, Carlsberg Chill, Carlsberg Light, Tuborg, and Kronenbourg 1664. These brands should work together to offer trade-up opportunities.

Fourth, they drove volume growth in Western China with improved sales and marketing projects. This included re-launching brands in Xinjiang, Yunnan and Ningxia.

Across the board, it was a strategy of regional dominance. They were building a competitive advantage based on local economies of scale in marketing, distribution and production. And they were racing to become a giant in the West.

Sunny was appointed CEO of Carlsberg China in 2006. In 2012, he became Chairman for Greater China. By 2013, he had taken Carlsberg China from one brewery in Huizhou to 39 breweries across seven provinces with over 11,000 China employees.

In 2010, Carlsberg became the largest shareholder in Chongqing Brewery, which has 16 breweries in Chongqing, Sichuan, Hunan, Anhui and Zhejiang. Carlsberg's goal was to expand the Shancheng brand, a leading brand in these markets. For most companies, going to Chongqing would be considered a big move West. For Carlsberg, it was actually a move East.

Today, according to Carlsberg, they have over 50 China breweries and over 60% market share in Western China, where beer consumption has been growing at 12% annually (versus 4-5% nationally). Carlsberg is also currently building its second largest brewery in the world. This $782M facility will have a production capacity of 10M hectoliters a year. And it will be located in Yunnan, China.

***

KEY POINT 4: BEER IN CHINA IS EVOLVING INTO A "GIANTS AND DWARVES" SITUATION

The Carlsberg story has a lot of good lessons about both Chinese consumers and competition. And it has a particularly interesting twist related to government.

First, Inland consumers are an important demographic. And beer, which was already uniformly drunk across China, is a product that nicely overcomes some of the Inland challenges (lower incomes, difficult to supply, more value focused, etc.).

But it is the competition here that is really interesting. In China, like everywhere else, mass-market beer is brewed, marketed and distributed locally, or at least regionally. It is not a product you ship from afar due to the weight and transportation costs (at least the mass-market version isn't). And it is a product where you are highly dependent on local wholesalers and retailers to stock and promote your brand. If you don't have significant market share in a local region, you will not be one of the 5-7 beers the local store carries. Overall, the economics of beer are regional.

What you typically see in the beer industry is a "Giants and Dwarves" situation. There are a couple of big beer companies that dominate (the Giants). And then there are a bunch of smaller companies (the Dwarves). Investment bankers and CEOs refer to this as "consolidation". Investors and economists call it "local economies of scale". Warren Buffett calls it "survival of the fattest." But basically when the Giants get so much bigger than the Dwarves, they can outspend them on fixed costs such as breweries, marketing and distribution. It becomes very difficult to take market share from them. And you see this situation in beer in most places in the world.

For example, between 1945 and 1985, the top five US brewers increased their combined US market share from about 20% to 70%. This was mostly the result of larger brewers increasing their spending on key fixed costs such as advertising, plants and distribution – exactly the things the smaller companies could not match. Spending on advertising, for instance, increased from 2% to 10% of sales. By 1985, it was a Giants and Dwarves situation, with Anheuser-Busch and Miller capturing market shares of 37% and 20% respectively. And this all occurred while US beer consumption was growing from 86M to over 200M hectoliters per year.

Giants and Dwarves
(photo by ArtFamily/Shutterstock)

This is somewhat counterintuitive. Beer should be a relatively fair fight. It's not that hard operationally. There are no technological advantages. There are no special sources of barley or hops. And consumers aren't particularly loyal to brands. It seems a level playing field. But in fact, it is an industry where you can build powerful competitive advantages over time. And this is exactly what has been happening in China since 1980. Four giant brewers have emerged to control over 60% of the Chinese market. However, in China there are three important differences to note.

First, almost all the Chinese beer giants are State-owned enterprises.

The four giants that have emerged are Tsingtao, China Resources (which makes Snow), Yanjing Beer and AB-InBev. Collectively, they had 63% of China's beer sales in 2013. The first three are State-owned, although China Resources does have a JV with SABMilller.

Second, prices for mainstream Chinese beer are pretty low.

People are used to paying low prices for beer. It is expected to be easily affordable to virtually everyone, regardless of income. For example, in 2013 AB-InBev had a global average EBITDA of 39.8% and SAB Miller had 31.3%. But in China, AB-InBev's 2013 EBITDA was 16.3%.

Third, the market is still less developed than in the West.

The top four brewers hold about 60% of the market (versus about 80% in the US). So the market hasn't consolidated completely yet.

We will talk more about these differences, but Giants and Dwarves is a good mental image for this situation. Giants and Dwarves is the middle-left of the China Consumer Pyramid. It is a situation where you can have a competitive advantage (unlike Operational Marathon) and the State is not an active force, beyond normal regulation (similar to Operational Marathon). It can be a protected and very profitable place to be. If an Operational Marathon is a situation to be wary of (or psychologically prepared for), Giants and Dwarves is a situation to be excited about (assuming you're a Giant).

For those who want to know more about this situation, please refer to the Appendix.

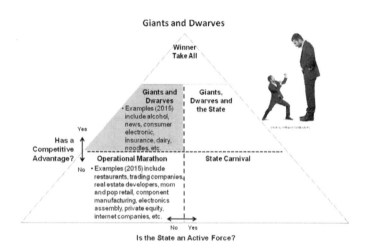

Giants and Dwarves

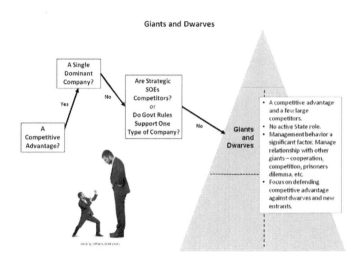

Giants and Dwarves

KEY POINT 5: GOVERNMENT-RELATED CAPABILITIES AND ASSETS CAN LEAD TO REAL COMPETITIVE ADVANTAGES

Question: Why are most all the China beer giants SOEs?

You can note in the below chart that the Chinese beer market looks similar to the rest of the world's, with a handful of companies dominating. So why are they SOEs in China? We just argued that beer is not an active government industry. In fact, the government really doesn't care who wins in beer. It turns out how this happened is an important lesson about the differences between international and State capitalism.

Most every region is dominated by beer giants, but in China they are SOEs

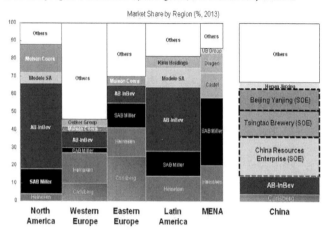

Market Share by Region (%, 2013)

Source: Data from Euromonitor 2013

Post-opening, the Chinese beer industry has grown and consolidated towards a Giants and Dwarves situation, just like everywhere else. Globally, the beer industry has consolidated to 10 companies accounting for 63% of volume – an increase from 42% in 2002.

But in China, there was a legacy of State-owned and State-run breweries that had been built across the country over the previous 40 years. It turns out that State-owned brewers are a lot better at acquiring other State-owned breweries. They had certain strengths in doing these deals, in financing them and in getting them approved. And those strengths proved decisive over time. SOE brewers got bigger a lot faster. This resulted in regional dominance and real competitive advantages (i.e., local economies of scale).

So beer, an industry in which the State has little interest (perhaps employment and a few brands), has ended up being dominated by companies that are State-owned anyway. And while these companies are State-owned, they actually operate almost entirely commercially (we call them "commercial SOEs").

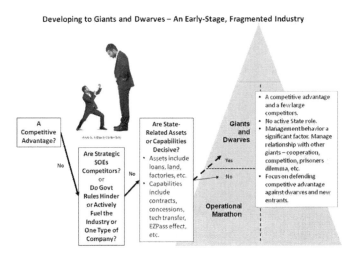

Developing to Giants and Dwarves – An Early-Stage, Fragmented Industry

We argue that the State impacts competition and industry structure in developing economy-State capitalism by five mechanisms (detailed in Chapter 3 and in the Appendix). Two of the five mechanisms are **State-Related Assets** (land, capital, breweries, etc.) and **State-Related Capabilities** (merger approvals, technology transfer, contracting and concessions, etc.). While these are not competitive advantages, they impact the competitive dynamics over time. And sometimes they prove decisive. In this case, they helped SOEs get to economies of scale faster, which was decisive.

Jeff calls this the "EZPass lane" (for those not familiar with EZPass in the US, it's an RFID tag for cars that lets you drive through toll booths without stopping). Think of business in China as a series of highways covered with toll booths. You drive about a mile and then you have to stop at a toll booth. You wait for the person to let you through. And usually you pay a fee. Then you continue on and likely hit another tollbooth pretty fast. In some sectors in China, you are constantly stopping in this way. You must stop to get approvals to use your money, to open a new branch, to file taxes, to pay business expenses, to hire staff and for lots of other things. China is often rightfully referred to as a "nation of licenses". It's also one of the reason guanxi (i.e., knowing the toll booth guy) matters. But if you get your approvals faster than your competitors, you can sometimes have an advantage. You can open branches faster. You can bring goods into the country faster. You can access loans easier. And, importantly, you can do mergers and acquisitions faster. It's like having an EZPass lane at the toll booth. You go through a fast lane while everyone else waits in line.

SOEs do have an EZPass lane for some things, relative to private and/or foreign companies. In some industries, this strength doesn't matter (i.e., operating restaurants). But in other situations, such as in acquiring SOE breweries in a rapidly consolidating beer industry, it can make a decisive difference.

This is how commercially focused SOEs have come to dominate beer in China. It has not happened through explicit licensing or some government-granted competitive advantages, nor through any particular policy. In fact, outside of taxes, the government seems not to have much interest in the beer sector. It was a unique SOE strength that enabled them to get to scale faster than private companies. Plus they were first movers, which helped. The takeaway here is that **commercial SOEs can compete and win in private markets**.

FINAL POINT: INLAND CHINA IS LIKELY THE LAST GREAT BATTLEGROUND FOR MULTINATIONALS

There aren't that many emerging markets left. It is likely that Inland China and its +200M consumers will be the last really big frontier for multinationals. If so, here is some advice for going West today.

- You will need a product that can be sold at a low price point. As mentioned, Inland consumers have lower incomes and are more value focused.

- You will need a product that can be distributed across a massive and underdeveloped geography. Beer does well Inland as a consumable. And it turns out there is an existing infrastructure of breweries across the Inland that is a legacy of the State-run economy days.

- Finally, you will want an industry that has attractive and profitable competitive dynamics, likely "Giants and Dwarves".

For Carlsberg, going for dominant market share in Inland China was both very smart and actually doable. Looking forward, we can probably expect to see the following by Carlsberg and other China brewers:

- Continued acquisitions of controlling stakes in breweries in select provinces.

- Establishment of strategic alliances in select provinces in order to become a dominant player.

- Creation of an optimal brand portfolio to capture consumers in all different segments.

- Focus on premiumization in order to improve margins.

A good final number to keep mind when thinking about Inland consumers is 670M. That is the number of people who used to live on under $1 per day in China (mostly in the countryside) and who are now are in the middle class (or on the way). This movement of 670M people out of poverty and into the middle class is one of China's greatest achievements. And it makes one pretty optimistic about the future of Inland China.

Inland China includes fantastic places like Fenghuang in Western Hunan
(photo by Hung Chung Chih / Shutterstock)

CHAPTER #3:
HOW WEALTHY CHINESE ARE SEDUCING CHRISTIE'S AND SOTHEBY'S

In March 2014, the new Long Museum opened in Shanghai. At 33,000 square meters, it is now officially China's largest private museum. And much of its collection has come from its husband and wife founders Liu Yiqian and Wang Wei, who are semi-officially known as China's "art super-collectors".

Wang Wei and Liu Yiqian are worth paying attention to. They have risen from middle class backgrounds to become two of China's wealthiest people. And now, like the Gettys and the Guggenheims of the West, they are opening museums to house their personal art collection. The opening show at the Long Museum featured more than 300 pieces by over 200 artists – and many were taken from the founders' personal collection.

Liu Yiqian has also made headlines recently with his purchase of one of the famous Ming Dynasty "chicken cups". These 500-year-old tea cups have pictures of poultry on them (hence the name) and are regarded as the "holy grail" of Chinese porcelain. Only 17 are known to exist and Yiqian recently paid $36M for one at a Sotheby's auction in Hong Kong. He paid by swiping his American Express card 24 times ($1.5M per swipe?) and then, to some degree of controversy, drank tea from the cup.

Art super-collector Liu Yiqian and his Ming Dynasty chicken cup
(photo by ImagineChina)

This chapter is about China's emerging affluent consumers. These are the newly wealthy, or at least newly comfortable, consumers that have discovered that there are lots of nice things to buy in the world – such as nice cars in Beijing and nice apartments in New York. And the Chinese art market is being particularly fueled by their spending. (Note: Over 400 galleries and 700 museums have been opened in China in the last four years alone.)

This consumer group has, unsurprisingly, caught the attention of Christie's and Sotheby's, the world's premier art auction houses. This chapter will show how these prestigious companies are fighting for this consumer group – and are finding themselves challenged in the process. But first, some key points about China's emerging affluent consumers.

KEY POINT 1: AFFLUENT CONSUMERS ARE THE GREAT WALL OF CHINESE MONEY

Thanks to a historically rapid industrialization, China has fairly quickly produced about 150 billionaires. These are the super-wealthy that often make the newspapers (Jeff refers to them as "moody money"). They are an interesting group but the much more important group are the affluent (i.e., the regularly wealthy) Chinese consumers. This group is less high profile but far greater in number.

We define affluent Chinese consumers as those with over $46,000 in annual household income. That gives them about the same spending power as Americans making over $100,000 per household. There were 4.5M of these households in 2010, but this is expected to increase to 20M by 2020. There is also an upper middle class immediately below this affluent group that is defined as making $25,000-$46,000 per household per year. This group will number about 80M by 2020. This group also tends to grow into the affluent so it is worth keeping an eye on both. Basically, a great wall of Chinese money is about to hit the rest of the world.

CHINA'S AFFLUENT ARE YOUNG, UNDERLEVERAGED AND CONFIDENT

About 80% of China's wealthy are under age 45. This compares to 30% in the US and only 19% in Japan. In China, the economic takeoff really began in the 1990's so people born in the 1970's had a huge leg up on their parents. The Cultural Revolution, which ended in 1976 and effectively killed a generation's earning prospects.

The young affluent do tend to buy different things. Travel and active recreation receive more of their spending. Even spending within product segments tends to be different. For example, Lancôme, now the largest cosmetics company in China, focuses more on products for the early prevention of skin aging in China.

China's affluent are also among the world's most underleveraged consumers. Less than 50% of homes purchased in China use leverage. And overall household debt to income is less than 50%. While this has recently increased significantly, it is far less than the 90-110% seen in the US. So they have a lot of unused spending power in reserve.

Finally, this is a group that is extremely confident about the future. Over 70% think their household income will increase significantly in the next 5 years. This compares to less than 50% in the US. There are good reasons for this optimism as urban income has been growing at over 10% annually for the last decade. If you were part of this, you'd be pretty optimistic too.

Generally speaking, China's affluent are really just getting started on their spending. Hangzhou now has as many wealthy households as Atlanta (adjusted for purchasing power parity). Foshan has as many wealthy households as Denver. And just wait until this group starts having more kids.

China's affluent are young, underleveraged and confident.
(photo by Igor Demchenkov/Shutterstock)

KEY POINT 2: CHINESE ARE THE WORLD'S LEADING BUYERS OF LUXURY GOODS

China's consumers account for over a third of worldwide luxury consumption (fashion ready-to-wear, shoes, hand-bags, watches, fine jewelry, etc.). Chinese consumption of luxury goods is now up to about $100B annually. That's a good "China is big" number to remember. And this luxury consumption has been growing annually at about 15%, more than double the rate of the global market. However, this does vary a lot year to year.

Luxury consumption is somewhat synonymous with affluent consumers. People tend to equate the two. But Chinese luxury consumption is actually much broader than this. Luxury buying and other types of "affluent spending behavior" are also happening at lower income levels. Everyone is getting more sophisticated and is spending bigger money. Lower income groups just buy luxury more episodically.

This increasing sophistication is creating an important battle between luxury and mainstream brands. Mainstream brands mostly own China's customers today and are struggling to develop credibility in luxury. They are trying to rise with their customers. In contrast, luxury brands are struggling to create a lower entry point that enables the middle class to buy occasionally. They can usually pull people once but have difficulty retaining and scaling them. This luxury-mainstream brand battle is fascinating and evolving quickly right now.

KEY POINT 3: AFFLUENT CHINESE HAVE DISCOVERED THE WORLD IS FULL OF COOL STUFF TO BUY

In the last several years, affluent Chinese have started traveling, and there has been a frenzy of overseas buying. This has included everything from French art and luxury Italian handbags to California wine and Toronto homes. In 2014, the overseas asset of choice was Western real estate.

A couple of generalizations on this:

CHINESE ARE A BIG FORCE IN GLOBAL TOURISM AND OVERSEAS LUXURY

The Chinese have recently overtaken the Americans as the world's biggest tourist spenders. And Europe is now their second most popular destination, behind Hong Kong/Macau. During the Chinese New Year celebrations, you won't see more dragons anywhere in Europe than at the Galeries Lafayette in Paris.

Total Chinese luxury spending has averaged about 50/50 inside and outside of China (although overseas has increased a lot recently). And almost 13% say they buy luxury products exclusively overseas. The top stated reasons for buying overseas are to get the latest products and to be assured of top quality. This also has to do with import tariffs and the RMB being a strong and appreciating currency. Chinese import tariffs on luxury goods (plus value added tax plus consumption tax) add up to a 40%+ premium at home. In 2011, China beat out Russia as the top nationality at duty-free shopping globally (about 17%).

It's also worth noting that China's global shoppers are not just interested in luxury products. They also like services. Mei Zhang, the founder of Beijing's high-end travel operator WildChina, offers family holidays to destinations such as Kenya, Patagonia and Alaska at $10,000 per head. Chinese are now the third largest group landing in Antarctica, where they zip around in Zodiac inflatables and watch penguins.

WINE IS A GATEWAY DRUG FOR GLOBAL ASSET PURCHASES

There is a collision of expensive wine and affluent Chinese currently happening in Hong Kong. It is one of those quirks of global business. Wealthy Chinese are buying expensive wine, both for drinking and investment. And for various Mainland regulatory reasons, this is mostly happening in Hong Kong through auctions, special investment companies and other means. So we are seeing auctions, wine-focused asset management companies and even special wine storage facilities around Victoria Island. It's all pretty entertaining.

And Chinese buying wine often end up traveling to the wine regions. So the number of Chinese staying in Burgundy, France jumped from approximately 38,000 in 2010 to over 70,000 in 2011. And this led to real estate purchases. Wealthy Chinese are now buying homes and vineyards in the South of France and in the California Napa Valley. According to Safer, of the 35 châteaux with vineyards that sold in Bordeaux in 2011, 21 went to Chinese buyers. It turns out that wine is a kind of gateway drug for global assets.

WESTERN EDUCATIONS ARE PARTICULARLY POPULAR WITH THE AFFLUENT

Chinese students are now, by far, the largest group of foreign students on U.S. campuses. According to the Institute of International Education, their numbers jumped 21% in 2013, reaching 235,597. In England, there are now almost as many Chinese students as British ones doing full-time postgraduate master's degrees. It turns out a Western degree is something affluent Chinese really want for their kids - and this also fuels real estate purchases.

AFFLUENT CHINESE ARE CRAZY ABOUT FOREIGN REAL ESTATE

In 2013, the US became the #1 target for outbound Chinese real estate investment. Chinese buyers bought approximately $11B worth of US properties. This was about 12% of all US real estate bought by foreigners, up from 5% in 2007. California is currently the most popular location for Chinese buyers, but this changes pretty frequently.

The reasons for these real estate purchases are mixed. Many are buying foreign homes as a store of wealth. It's somewhere safe to put your money. Some are buying because it's cheaper than Chinese real estate, which is overheated right now. But the most common reason is that buying US real estate is a way to get their child into a top US school. A Hong Kong woman recently paid

$6.5M for a two-bedroom apartment in New York City. The apartment is for when her daughter attends Harvard or Columbia. The daughter is currently two years old.

Luxury apartments on Hong Kong's peak are particularly popular real estate targets. (photo by leungchopan/Shutterstock)

THE STORY OF CHRISTIE'S AND SOTHEBY'S IN CHINA

Okay. Back to Chinese art and our story for this chapter.

In September 2013, premier art auction house Christie's held its first-ever auction in China. They have had a representative office in Shanghai since 1994. And they have been running auctions out of Hong Kong for decades. But this small auction (about $25M) was their first in the Mainland.

Shortly thereafter, on December 1, 2013, Sotheby's held its first major auction in China. This 141-item Beijing auction broke records for six artists, including Chinese-French abstract painter Zao Wou-ki and Chinese realist painter, Li Guijun. Sotheby's, unlike Christie's, currently operates in China with a JV partner, State-owned Beijing Gehua Cultural Development Group. In both cases, Christie's and Sotheby's were on the home turf of major Chinese auction houses for the first time. And this was really the culmination of a 45-year journey to China for both companies.

A bit of background.

Sotheby's was founded in London in 1744. Christie's was founded shortly after in 1766. In the nearly 250 years since, these two companies have controlled much of the premier art auction world. As recently as 2007, they had over 70% of the premier art and jewelry auctions between them. Their combined market share has fallen significantly in the last several years and is now closer to 40-50%. However, in 2013, Sotheby's alone still conducted 250 auctions at 90 locations in 40 countries.

And while the China art market is relatively new, these companies have been selling Chinese art successfully for decades. For example, in 1979, Wen Zhengming's Ming dynasty painting, "Master Liu's Garden," sold for the then surprising price of $121,000. And in 1980, Sotheby's hosted its first auction of modern Chinese paintings in Hong Kong.

Christie's and Sotheby's really began competing for Chinese art consignments in the early 1980's. At that time, most Chinese art was sourced outside of China, often from Europe. And because works were sold cross-border (Europe had few buyers of Chinese art), Chinese art sales were driven largely by auction houses rather than by galleries. Chinese art auctions did eventually centralize to Hong Kong over time. The best 19th- and 20th-century works were typically auctioned in Hong Kong, while more traditional Song, Yuan, Ming and Qing dynasty paintings were sold in New York. In 1989, Christie's recorded the first Chinese works to bring in $1M.

Some nice detail on a statue in the Forbidden City
(photo by Hung Chung Chih/Shutterstock)

This is all a fairly interesting historical confluence. Demand for Chinese art was blossoming at roughly the same time that China opened up to the world – and shortly before newly wealthy Chinese would transform the market. And all of this should have been good news for Christie's and Sotheby's, not unlike when wealthy Japanese and Saudi buyers entered the art scene. However, the Chinese art market has turned out to be a particularly difficult environment for them to navigate.

***

THESE ARE STILL THE WILD WEST DAYS OF CHINA'S ART MARKET

As reported in the TEFAF Art Market Report, the Chinese art market in 2012 was $13.7B, compared to $18.4B in the US. And from 2009 to 2011, Chinese art sales grew by 350%, with auctions approximately 70% of this. By that report's numbers, global market shares were 33% for the US and 25% for China. And the most popular type of Chinese art by value was painting and calligraphy, with 48% of the market in 2012. Ceramics and collectibles were 27%.

However, these numbers draw and deserve considerable criticism. Many of the sales recorded at Chinese auction houses are never collected. And fakes and forgeries are a significant problem. Also, there is evidence that auctions are being used as a front for bribery. Even the sale of Qi Baishi's famous "Eagle Standing on a Pine Tree" painting has come under fire, due to questions of authenticity. Plus, the art market in China has been declining from its peak in 2011. So all of this is pretty fuzzy.

Looking at individual artists gives you better numbers. In 2011, six of the top 10 artists by auction revenue were Chinese. Zhang Daqian (1899-1983), a traditionalist painter who spent much of his life in exile, came in first with $550M in sales. This was about $200M above both Andy Warhol and Pablo Picasso. Another big seller was Qi Baishi (1864-1957), whose work sold for $465M that year. For living artists, three of the 10 most expensive works sold in 2011 were Chinese. This included a work by painter Cui Ruzhuo that was purchased for $16M at a Christie's Hong Kong auction. Other current notable Chinese art stars are Zhang Xiaogang and Zeng Fanzhi.

So the China art market is definitely big and growing (more or less) – but there is still a lot of Wild West-type stuff going on. Counterfeiting is a significant problem. Paintings at auctions are frequently refused due to authenticity concerns. And in Hebei province in 2013, the government closed a new museum when it was reported that most of the works on display were fakes. And, of course, there is the famous village of Dafen.

THE VILLAGE "ART FACTORY" OF DAFEN

Dafen is a small section of Shenzhen, so it is not actually a village per se. But it is well known due to its annual production of about 100,000 paintings, most of which are copycats. It is a place where if you want an outstanding copy of a van Gogh or a Monet, you can get it in about two weeks and possibly for as little as 100 RMB. With more than 1,200 galleries packed into a few small city blocks, Dafen has aptly been called the epicenter of fake art.

Dafen began as an artists' colony, set up by a Hong Kong artist and dealer in 1989. Using migrant laborers, he and other artists began producing multiple copies of the same work, basically a factory approach. Dafen quickly became known as a place that could do high-quality, high-volume copies of masterpieces for export. And according to the Art Industry Association of Dafen, these exports eventually grew to a reported 1.2B RMB in sales per year. At its height, approximately 60% of the world's cheap oil paintings were coming from Dafen.

Since the financial crisis, the Dafen story has changed somewhat. Western paintings for tourists and exports have declined and Dafen's artists have shifted more toward works for domestic sale. This means mass-produced paintings for hotels and office buildings. If you have been in a three-star Chinese hotel, you have probably seen Dafen paintings on the walls.

Dafen is also a good symbol of the aforementioned counterfeiting problem in Chinese art. It's both pervasive and profitable. And this problem isn't limited to China. Recently in New York City, a 73-year-old Chinese immigrant artist was discovered to have created and sold at least 65 fake drawings and paintings to top New York galleries. His paintings had been presented as "newly discovered" works by artists like Jackson Pollock and Robert Motherwell. And they had been selling quite well in the US for years.

Other Wild West-type problems in the Chinese art market are speculation and price manipulation. Individual and small-group investors often buy items and resell them to other collectors quickly at a profit. And art investment funds are particularly motivated to inflate the value of their holdings. As reported by the New York Times, a work by Qi Baishi, "Fish and Shrimp," was sold four different times in a 10-year period, starting at $30,000 and peaking at $794,000, before later selling for $552,000.

It is clear that the discussed rising affluent Chinese consumers are fueling much of the current demand for Chinese art. And that is very attractive to Christie and Sotheby's. However all this Wild West behavior is another example of the ruthless competition that can quickly follow Chinese consumer spending. What is unique in this case is that Chinese art is very important to the Chinese government, so the State is also an active force in the market. Additionally, we are also seeing the emergence of two important Chinese auction houses that are becoming serious challengers to long-dominant Sotheby's and Christie's.

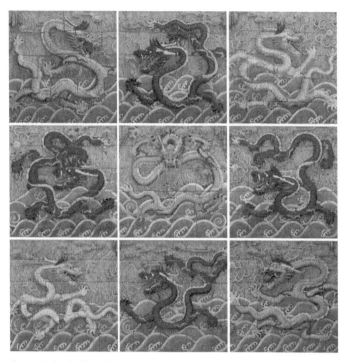

Some detail at the Forbidden City. The government is very active in historic Chinese art.
(photo by CaptainImages/Shutterstock)

THE STARTLINGLY RAPID RISE OF CHINA GUARDIAN AND POLY

The first major auction house to emerge in modern China was China Guardian. It was established in 1993 by Wang Yannan, the daughter of Zhao Ziyang, a former Premier of the PRC. And it was patterned after Christie's and Sotheby's (yet another art copycat). Guardian quickly became the largest auction house in China and specialized in traditional Chinese art forms, antiques and artifacts, as well as in modern and traditional Chinese painting. The important differences between Guardian and the Western giants were its national, not global, focus and its close connection to the Chinese government.

However, in 2005, China Guardian was eclipsed by the meteoric rise of State-owned Poly Culture. Poly Culture is part of the China Poly Group Corporation, a very large, 55% State-owned enterprise created by the State Council in 1992. Poly Group is one of the SOEs that every businessperson should know. The company started out selling weapons to the People's Liberation Army (Poly Technologies) and has since grown into a conglomerate covering real estate, automobiles, entertainment and many other sectors. For example, their publically traded real estate division, Poly Real Estate, is now one of the largest residential developers in China. After its launch in 2005 Poly Culture quickly became the largest auction house in China, with 75% turnover (2013) coming from Poly Auction Beijing and 25% coming from Poly Auction Hong Kong.

If Sotheby's and Christie's are purely commercial Giants (as defined in Chapter 2), then Poly Culture and Guardian are something else. They are certainly Giants, dominating the domestic art auction industry. But Poly in particular is also a direct extensions of the State. Because it turns out, what happens to historic Chinese art is a significant concern to the Chinese government. Part of this sensitivity is about repatriating works that were stolen and misappropriated over the centuries. Many of the works that have been returned can be seen on display at Poly's headquarters in Beijing.

Poly Auction is now not just one of the top two auction houses in China. It is also the number three art auction house in the world (after Christie's and Sotheby's). Their 2013 turnover was over a billion dollars (about one-fourth of Sotheby's). They sell approximately 10,000 objects each week, with as many as 40 different catalogs per show.

So we actually have two different types of auction giants pursuing affluent Chinese consumers. In the West, we have Sotheby's and Christie's, two dominant giants with strong competitive advantages (network economics). One is public and the other is private. And in China, we have Poly and Guardian, two dominant giants with strong competitive advantages (network economics plus active government support). One is public and the other is private. And these four companies are now coming into direct competition for the first time.

THE HIGHLY SYMBOLIC COLLISION OF SOTHEBY'S-CHRISTIE'S AND POLY-GUARDIAN

As mentioned, both Christie's and Sotheby's held their first auctions in Mainland China in late 2013. And that put them on the home turf of Poly and Guardian for the first time. Well, sort of. In the Mainland, foreign auction houses can only deal in watches, wine, jewelry and contemporary art - not Chinese antiques, classic Chinese paintings or other items from before 1911. This includes calligraphy and ancient works, the areas that Chinese collectors are most interested in. So it's not completely direct competition yet. But it's close and it's really symbolic.

Because at the same time, Poly and Guardian have been expanding internationally. And they are now on Sotheby's and Christie's home turf for the first time. Both have moved into Hong Kong. And Poly is now moving aggressively into New York City, where Sotheby's is headquartered. Thus far, they have focused mostly on finding consignments in the US for sale in China, particularly Chinese collectibles. But Poly's openly stated ambition is to become the world's top art auction house. According to CEO Jiang Yingchun, "We are very big in the art auction market in Mainland China but still have a long way to go to become the biggest auction house worldwide".

So rising affluent Chinese are causing a fascinating competition – State-backed Chinese auction houses versus private international auction houses. It's a symbolic fight between Chinese State capitalism and international capitalism. How this will play out is not clear.

Guardian and Poly are searching for Chinese antiquities in the West to sell in China and Hong Kong. But Sotheby's and Christie's have been developing their pipelines for such consignments for decades. Additionally, they have relationships with collectors and other sources of Western art that also appeal to Chinese buyers. This includes artists such as Picasso, Monet, and Rembrandt. The Chinese giants, on the other hand, dominate in China and have better access to works by rising contemporary Chinese artists, dealers and collectors.

So it's not clear who will win. And this re-raises the three factors at the center of this book: customers versus competition versus the role of the State. All three are important in this situation.

KEY POINT 4: CHINESE ART AUCTIONS ARE A "GIANTS, DWARVES AND THE STATE" SITUATION

Christie's and Sotheby's are an example of the Giants and Dwarves situation discussed in Chapter 2. Not only do the two companies have big market share, but they have had it for hundreds of years. Stable, long-term market share is pathognomonic for a sustainable competitive advantage.

But the rise of State-backed Poly and Guardian is challenging that. And in Chinese art, the State is an active force – shaping the industry, creating new competitors and acting in its own, often noneconomic, interests.

We call this situation "Giants, Dwarves and the State". It is a variation of the Giants and Dwarves situation described for Carlsberg and is quite common in China. We see it in automobiles, where State-owned manufacturers are actively supported. We see it in pharmaceuticals, banks and insurance. And it is very common in industrial and B2B businesses such as trains, airplanes, and energy (Chinese B2B competition is a topic for another book). In art auctions, strategic SOEs are direct competitors. And they are very different than the commercial SOEs described in beer. State support is actively for certain companies.

The State is both policeman and player in "Giants, Dwarves and the State"
(photo by Taras Vyshnya/Shutterstock)

Keep in mind, there are also approximately 350 smaller auction houses in China (up from about 100 in 2005). So we have Giants and the State, but we also have lots of Dwarves as well. So when we say State support is against certain players, that does not necessarily mean foreign companies. It impacts lots of private Chinese companies as well.

Giants, Dwarves and the State is the middle right of the pyramid. It is a situation where you have a competitive advantage and the State is an active force (our two main questions). Contrary to conventional wisdom, this can be a protected and very profitable place to be. But working effectively with the government is critical here. As Alibaba founder Jack Ma said at the 2015 Davos World Economic Forum, "I always say to my people 'fall in love with the government but don't marry them.'"

For those who want to know more about this situation, the Appendix also has our frameworks for the impact of the State on competition and industry structure.

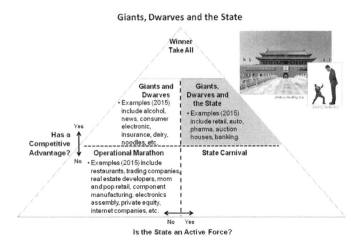

Giants, Dwarves and the State

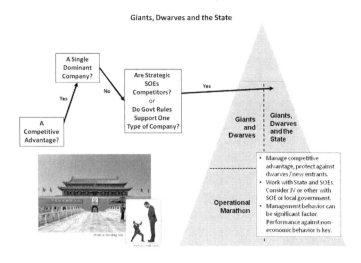

Giants, Dwarves and the State

The takeaways for this situation are **1) you can win big in China if you get the consumer AND the government.** And **2) State capitalism can be exceptionally profitable.**

For Sotheby's and Christie's, there is a domestic versus international network aspect that makes this situation less clear. You can actually see a similar dynamic in credit cards. China's State-backed credit card UnionPay has long benefited from its domestic payment network and a government-granted monopoly. MasterCard and Visa have an international network but, for the most part, not been allowed to sell cards in the Mainland credit card market. This is how UnionPay went from a start-up in 2002 to larger than Visa today in transactions. However, Visa and MasterCard are now starting to compete in China. And UnionPay has started to go international and into MasterCard/Visa territory. So it's definitely Giants, Dwarves and the State in China. But it is also another China network versus international network fight. We discuss this dynamic more in the Appendix.

FINAL POINT: CHINA'S AFFLUENT CONSUMERS ARE ULTIMATELY ABOUT ASPIRATIONS AND TRADING UP

A lot of the story of affluent Chinese consumers (and Sotheby's and Christie's) is the pursuit of aspirations. Affluent Chinese want to improve themselves. They want to improve where they live. They want to improve how they are seen. And they now have the means to do so.

These aspirations show up as a "trading up" in purchases. Affluent consumers are buying everything from better whiskey to better furniture to better paintings. They are taking nicer vacations and sending their kids to better schools. Everything is being taken up a notch. For many companies, this means a market of increasing volumes is changing to a market of increasing prices. You sell nicer things instead of just more things. For example, sales of premium skin care products have grown at 20% for most of the past decade, compared with only 10% growth for more standard skin care products. Similarly, sales of SUVs are projected to grow at around 20%, annually while regular car growth is closer to 10%.

But there are still lots of value consumers in China as well. And there are also the new mainstream consumers we discussed. How do you appeal to aspiring up-traders, new mainstream consumers and value consumers at the same time? Is that even a good idea? This is a significant question for many companies in China today.

When in China, note how many different types of consumers and businesses there are on the same street. Modern office towers are right next to small retailers. Luxury condos are right next to old apartments with clothes drying on the balconies. Bicycles and scooters are next to cars. The different classes of Chinese consumers all live, by and large, right on top of each other.

New luxury stilt-houses on Hainan Island
(photo by Captain Yeo/Shutterstock)

CHAPTER #4:
HOW TO WIN AND LOSE IN THE WORLD'S LARGEST DEATH MARKET

At midnight on May 31, 2014, traditional land burials became illegal in the Eastern Chinese city of Anqing. The local government, faced with limited land and a large and growing elderly population, had passed an ordinance forbidding the practice. Cremation and other options were encouraged. Land burials without cremation were henceforth illegal.

But beliefs regarding burial, family and the afterlife run deep in China – from the fairly common desire for a lavish funeral to the yearly Qingming Jie holiday on which one visits their parents' graves. For example, in Anqing there is a tradition of constructing one's own coffin prior to death. The elderly will sometimes spend up to a decade working on their coffins, which are viewed as a quiet resting place after a hard life.

The new Anqing prohibition on both homemade coffins and non-cremated land burials became a national story when it was reported that an 81-year-old woman hung herself in order to beat the May 31 deadline.

And she was not alone. Her neighbor had starved himself to death earlier that month. Another elderly woman threw herself down a well. Another killed herself after authorities destroyed her coffin. A newspaper reported that six people had killed themselves to beat the deadline. The whole event resulted in media outrage across China.

We have argued that China's consumer stories are consumer, competition and government factors intertwined. But what happens when the interests of the State and consumers are in direct conflict? That is what happened in the city of Anqing. And that is what is happening in the world's largest deathcare market.

About nine million people die every year in China (approximately one million from smoking). But while the U.S. has over 10,000 cemeteries, China has only about 3,000. And by most estimates, the existing allocated burial space will be used up in about six years. So as the population ages and urbanization continues, more and more deaths are happening in cities, exactly where there is less and less land. The State has big concerns about this.

However, Chinese elderly are a growing consumer demographic. They have large numbers, increasing wealth and deep cultural preferences about things such as burials. And many of their preferences run directly opposite to the goals of the State. So at the same time the government is giving free boat trips to encourage burials at sea, middle class Chinese are buying up cemetery plots in a mini-real estate boom. At the same time consumers are holding elaborate funeral services in cities like Guangzhou, government officials are confiscating coffins in cities like Anqing and Xindian.

China has few churches, castles or mosques. Its most famous historical sites are tombs, such as the Terracotta Warriors and the Sun Yat-sen mausoleum (shown). (photo by Tropinina Olga / Shutterstock)

That is our key question for this chapter. **What happens when 190M elderly consumers have different goals than the State?** And how is Fu Shou Yuan, China's leading funeral company, managing this situation? But first a few points on elderly Chinese consumers.

KEY POINT 1: THE NUMBER OF ELDERLY CHINESE IS GROWING REALLY FAST

The number of elderly in China is, like everything else, really big. According to the National Bureau of Statistics, in 2013 China counted over 190M people above 60 years old, about 13% of the population. This is actually low as a percentage (US is 19%, Europe is 22% and Japan is above 30%). China's elderly are expected to increase to 24% by 2030. That would put it at the same percentage as most developed countries and would mean an increase to 345M people. So this population is growing really fast (about 5% per year). China will soon be the most aged of the BRIC countries and will have the largest elderly population on the planet.

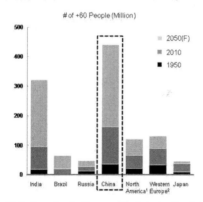

China will be the oldest BRIC country

Note: The three sections of each bar are cumulative. The top of each bar refers to the
      percentage of 60 years of age and above in the population,
      e.g., China has ~12% of population above 60 in year 2010 and ~34% in 2050
1 Data for North America includes Canada and United States only
2 Data for Western Europe includes Belgium, France, Germany, Ireland, Italy, Netherlands,
  Portugal, Spain and UK only

Source: chart recreated from Boston Consulting Group, data from UN Population Prospects 2010

This rapid increase in China's elderly is coming from two primary factors. First, people are dying later because of improvements in health. People are now dying from things like cancer and strokes, basically the same things that kill people in the developed world. Here's an unrelated factoid to ponder: China spends approximately 5% of what the US spends per person on healthcare and people live an average of 2 years longer.

Second, the birth rate is dropping so there are fewer young people. The one child policy has a lot to do with this, but it is mostly driven by urbanization and the associated income gains. Families generally get smaller as incomes rise. The one child policy has recently been loosened but these changes are unlikely to change China's declining birth rate in the near term.

Seniors are rising everywhere – but faster in China

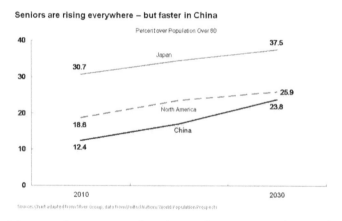

Source: Chart adapted from Silver Group, data from United Nations World Population Prospects

Most predictions are that the median age in China will increase from 35 to 37 years in the coming decade. That would put it about where the US is at 37.6. Most of the world is aging. China is just doing it faster as it catches up.

Note: this aging process isn't happening the same way in every city. By 2020, 20% of the population will be over 65 in six of China's city clusters. But in five other clusters, including Kunming and Shenzhen, over half the population will be under 35. Migrants and poverty have a lot to do with this.

By 2030, 345M Chinese will be over 60 years old.
(photo by Jack Q/Shutterstock)

KEY POINT 2: ELDERLY CHINESE CONSUMERS DON'T HAVE OR SPEND A LOT OF MONEY. BUT THEIR KIDS DO.

Elderly Chinese consumers are not wealthy. And this is a big difference from the wealth distribution of most other countries. Note in the below chart, elderly Chinese have earned less and tend to save more than just about any other demographic.

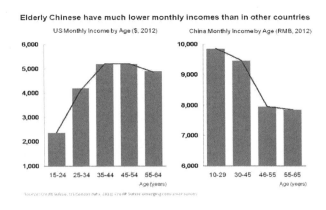

Elderly Chinese have much lower monthly incomes than in other countries

US Monthly Income by Age ($, 2012)   China Monthly Income by Age (RMB, 2012)

Source: Credit Suisse; US Census data, 2012; Credit Suisse emerging consumer survey

This is unsurprising given most people in China over age 55-60 had many working years during the Cultural Revolution (1966-1976). Many educated youth spent their first decade in the workforce feeding pigs and such. This gave them colorful stories but little wealth and few marketable skills. Those that did find their way back to the cities often wound up in State enterprises. This was also not a big opportunity for wealth creation, especially after Zhu Rongji got through laying off a good 20% of this group in the 1990s. This generation simply doesn't have wealth like the generations that have followed.

These experiences have also engrained in the Chinese elderly a visceral frugality, not unlike the generation of Americans who lived through the Great Depression. A 2011 McKinsey survey showed Chinese ages 55-65 in first-tier cities spend about half their expenditures on food and very little on discretionary categories. For example, only 7% of senior spending went to apparel. However, those who were just 10 years younger spent 38% on food and 13% on apparel. So if your business is selling something to elderly Chinese, keep in mind they don't have a lot of money and they generally won't spend it anyway.

When thinking about elderly Chinese consumers it is useful to combine them with their children, who have more money and a willingness to spend it on their parents. Back in 2006, Boston Consulting Group reported that 59% of Chinese elderly lived with their relatives. And many of the remaining 41% were dependent financially on their families.

That said, there is going to be increasingly more spending in the elderly segment going forward. The historical anomaly will disappear and incomes will then grow faster than other groups'. But today this is a tough market. Dreams of selling millions of nutrition drinks and senior housing units in China have mostly not come true.

Elderly Chinese are not yet the attractive consumer demographic everyone thinks they are.
(photo by szefei/Shutterstock)

KEY POINT 3: THE AGING OF CHINA HAS FAR-REACHING CONSEQUENCES

China is now in transition, shifting from a younger to an older society. However, the GDP per capita is still quite low and China is going to be old before it is rich. This aging-but-still-poor situation has interesting consequences. For example, at sporting venues throughout China you can often see about 40% of the seats filled with elderly bused from retirement homes by local governments.

CHINA TODAY HAS THE MOST FAVORABLE DEMOGRAPHICS IT WILL EVER HAVE.

For most of the past 30 years, the country has had a fairly young population with a large workforce. And there were more workers than retired people. This situation increased production and decreased overall costs, a sort of "demographic dividend".

But within the next year or so, this will end. The working-age population will start to decline for the first time. And the numbers of those over 60-65 will grow. In an interesting coincidence, the China Pavilion built for the 2010 Shanghai Expo bears a striking similarity to China's demographic future.

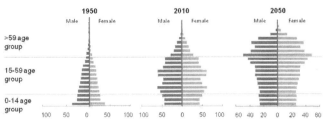

China's population continues to age rapidly

Source: UN population prospects 2010 revision, adapted from Boston Consulting Group

China's 2010 Expo Pavilion – and its demographic future.
(photo by m00osfoto / Shutterstock)

"4-2-1" FAMILY STRUCTURES ARE A PROBLEM IN AN AGING SOCIETY.

In the past, elderly Chinese could rely on their families and their village. Everyone looked out for the elderly. However, in urban China the village is gone and families are much smaller. So a common situation is the much discussed "4-2-1" family structure, where one child supports two parents and four grandparents. In a rapidly aging society, this "4-2-1" structure is a problem. It creates a financial burden for children and it also highlights the lack of other institutions and structures for the elderly to rely on. For example, there is really no government or private payment system for elderly care. And there are few nursing homes, public or private. "4-2-1" is only part of the problem.

AN AGING SOCIETY ALSO CREATES OPPORTUNITIES.

China's aging situation is resulting in some interesting innovations. One example is "eldergartens", which are basically daycare centers for seniors. In the morning, urban families take their elderly parents to these health-care/community centers. They then go to work and collect their parents again at the end of the day. These eldergartens target the gap between the government-funded nursing homes, which give priority to the disabled, the low-income and those with no family; and traditional nursing homes, which are often far out in the suburbs. Eldergartens provide social activities but also have general practitioners, pharmacists and nutritionists on site.

Our point is that the aging of China's society is far broader and transformative than just an increase in the number of elderly consumers. And the implications are still mostly unknown.

***

THE STORY OF WANG JISHENG AND FU SHOU YUAN

Okay. Back to deathcare and our story for this chapter.

It does not escape our attention that this is a somewhat morbid topic. And it is somewhat impolite for us to talk about it in a detached and businesslike fashion. But we wanted an industry that was emotional for consumers. And also where State involvement was active but not driven by economics. If beer drinking is unemotional and without serious State concerns, how people die is the inverse. Taking care of dead bodies might be the oldest job on earth. And it is a business deeply embedded in culture, economics, society, family and religion.

In 2014, there was a lot of discussion about the China deathcare market and how big it could be. For example, in the US, about 2.6M die per year and funerals are a $20B annual industry. This has created several very large public companies, including Service Corporation International, which in 2014 had about 12% of the market and a $4.7B market capitalization. Another example is StoneMor Partners L.P., which operates 303 US cemeteries and has a $750M market capitalization. So there is, morbidly, a lot of business excitement about the potential of the Chinese deathcare industry.

Burial and funeral services company Fu Shou Yuan is the most talked-about deathcare company in China today. They have been operating for 20 years and recently went public in Hong Kong (which provided a nice look into deathcare financials).

The person behind Fu Shou Yuan is Wang Jisheng. A graduate of Anhui Normal University, Jisheng came of age during the Cultural Revolution and most reports say he worked as a teacher and a counselor in Jiqing, Anhui. However, with the opening of China in 1979, Jisheng followed the path of many young men at that time. He moved to Shanghai and became a teacher at the Institute of Foreign Trade. From there he became a business manager. In this, his path was similar to those of Wang Shi and Ren Zhengfu, two of China's most well-known billionaires (we profiled them in our previous book). Wang and Ren spent the 1970's in government jobs, moved to Shenzhen in the early 1980's and then took positions that put them in the catbird seat for opportunities in China's boom days. They then started their own businesses in the late 1980's, which became China Vanke and Huawei.

Jisheng made a similar move in 1994. According to Want China Times, he became interested in the funeral business after reading an investment project that showed a burial company in Shanghai could make $1.6M a year by selling 50,000 plots at $500 a piece, basically a real estate play. And his stated motivation was the large and growing population of elderly people in China. But, by most accounts, his new business, named Fu Shou Yuan, did not meet expectations and was slow to take off.

After a few slow years and some struggling, his fortunes then began to change. In June 1996, Yu Cunshun, a well-known Shanghai explorer, died on an expedition in Xinjiang. Fu Shou Yuan organized a photo memorial for him that ended up raising $62,000 in donations for his family. Yu's family asked for his cremated remains to be buried at Fu Shou Yuan's primary cemetery in Shanghai.

In the next year, the company's annual revenue jumped 10-fold to $4.5M. It turns out celebrity and publicity are significant parts of the Chinese cemetery business. Within five years, Fu Shou Yuan's Shanghai cemetery would come to hold over 600 Chinese celebrities, including politicians, opera singers and actors.

However, it would still be another 13 years before Fu Shou Yuan went public. It turns out funerals and burials in China have some unique complications, such as:

- China's urbanization trend makes traditional cemeteries difficult. Available land is shrinking and urban living spaces are getting smaller. (One interesting but unrelated consequence of this is people are moving into taller buildings. The Chinese population today is about 10 meters higher in the air than it was a decade ago – literally rising Chinese consumers).

- Increasing income disparities are becoming an issue. A traditional burial with plot in Shanghai today can cost anywhere from $6,000 to $80,000 (the average cost in the US is $7,300, according to the National Funeral Directors Association). Rising burial plot costs in particular have led to the complaint that in modern China you "can't afford to live, can't afford to die."

- And, most importantly, much of what consumers want runs counter to the government's goals.

How to deal with these complications and how the Chinese deathcare industry would develop were important questions for Fu Shou Yuan. And, ironically, some of the answers were found in Chinese weddings.

WHAT CHINESE WEDDINGS CAN TEACH US ABOUT CHINESE FUNERALS

China is somewhat known for lavish marriages. And there is definitely a demographic that views such occasions as on opportunity to display wealth. For example, Cathy Tsui and Martin Lee KaShing spent an estimated $90M on their marriage in Australia in 2006, with a 5-carat diamond ring and a private jet for the groom's family. This can be viewed as vanity, fun or perhaps aspects of Chinese culture that are more demonstrative. But such stories do make the press on a regular basis.

Lavish Chinese wedding processions are not uncommon.
(photo by ImagineChina)

Every year, more than 10M couples get married in China and this creates an estimated $80B industry. Walk into any mall and you will find wedding photography services, wedding dress shops, wedding cake providers, wedding jewelry boutiques, and wedding honeymoon agents. It is not uncommon for Chinese fiancées take pictures with sumptuous costumes, Champagne, horses, and even castles (usually just cardboard cutouts). The price of a session can range from several thousand to several hundred thousand RMB.

You also see a lot of differentiation in Chinese weddings. For example, in Shandong, 1.5 kilos of 100-RMB bills are a common wedding present. In Inner Mongolia, wedding presents are often in the form of cattle or goats in multiples of nine, which sounds like "forever" in Mandarin. In Beijing, China's top luxury liquor, maotai, is a standard gift. In Shanghai, which is the country's most expensive city for marriage, a gift of 100,000 RMB and an apartment is common. At the opposite extreme, Chongqing bachelors often persuade their in-laws to let them off the hook with no gifts.

Funerals appear to be developing along the same line as weddings. First, we are now starting to see lavish burials that mimic lavish weddings. An example is the entrepreneur who paid an estimated 6M RMB for his mother's funeral in the city of Wenling. The funeral had a marching band, gold-painted cannons, gigantic screens and a fleet of nine Lincoln limos to accompany the deceased along a white-flowered path. A thousand mourners were there to commemorate the deceased (or possibly just to watch the spectacle).

Lavish funerals are becoming increasingly common.
(photo by ImagineChina)

Second, funerals for the middle class appear to be matching the wedding industry's approach of differentiated services but not uniform extravagance. Similar to wedding photography and different regional customs, we are starting to see a broad range of elegant, but not lavish, services and products. And Wang Jisheng appears to have integrated these aspects into Fu Shou Yuan.

FU SHOU YUAN GOES FOR DIFFERENTIATED SERVICES PLUS LUXURY REAL ESTATE

If celebrity was one important part of the Fu Shou Yuan equation, then differentiated services and premier real estate turned out to be the others. Fu Shou Yuan's cemetery in Shanghai is a prime location (feng shui matters) and the landscaping has made it more like a park than a cemetery. It has spectacular manicured lawns and running water. For burial plots, it offers personalized headstones and sculptures, even busts of the family member. Headstones are regularly polished and the landscaping is impeccable. They have even built large mausoleums with themed rooms, requiring key cards to enter.

The company also offers a wide range of differentiated services – everything from special landscaping to funeral catering. Funeral ceremonies can last for days, with some families hiring people to grieve around the clock. Offerings for the deceased can include everything from incense and fake money to iPads and luxury handbags. The grave of one former pop star even continually plays her most famous songs through a speaker.

Today, Fu Shou Yuan has cemeteries in Shanghai, Chongqing, Jinan, Hefei and Zhengzhou. In 2013, revenues reached $100M. According to Euromonitor, China's deathcare industry is now worth over $15B, and is predicted to grow 17% per year until 2017 (when the number of deaths is forecast to rise to 10.4M a year).

Wang Jisheng is now the head of the largest funeral company in the world's most populous nation. He is a renowned figure in the PRC deathcare industry and his profile has only increased with Fu Shou Yuan's recent Hong Kong IPO. And during all this, he has remained a teacher as well. He has been giving courses on cemetery management at the China Funeral Association since 1999.

Chinese cemeteries now offer personal tombs (location, location, location).
(photo by think4photop/Shutterstock)

So in Chinese funerals, we have several economic phenomena – a large and increasing population of elderly consumers, urbanization and real estate. That is a powerful combination. And there is a mini real estate boom happening in this market as well. For example, in Guangzhou a two-square-meter burial plot can cost $6,000-$16,000, up from about $1,000-$2,000 just five years ago. It is joked that Guangzhou housing agents rent houses during the day and sell graves at night.

And that brings us back to our original question: What happens when the interests of consumers and the State are in opposition? Or to phrase it differently, if there are all these powerful China phenomena in this industry, why isn't Fu Shou Yuan a lot bigger?

Fu Shou Yuan is the market leader. But after 20 years of operations, it is still only at six cemeteries, five funeral facilities and about $100M in revenue (2013). Although revenue is now increasing significantly it is still quite small relative to other China companies. Compare this to Service Corporation International in the US, which has 514 cemeteries and 16,000 funeral service locations. Or compare this to the market-leading companies founded by Wang Shi and Ren Zhengfu around the same time as Wang Jisheng founded Fu Shou Yuan. Both China Vanke and Huawei have revenues in the tens of billions. Why isn't market leader Fu Shou Yuan much, much bigger?

KEY POINT 4: CHINA'S DEATHCARE INDUSTRY IS A "TREADMILL"

Our answer to this question is that deathcare has, by and large, sat out the modernization of China. The market is inefficient, fragmented and underdeveloped. The players today are mostly small private companies and small State-run facilities. The largest company, Fu Shou Yuan, has only six cemeteries.

The critical factor here is the role of the State. Through multiple avenues, the State has kept the industry undeveloped, the players small and the services limited. In developed countries, cemetery businesses are naturally fragmented, but there is usually a mix of small local operators and large national companies (usually public). China's situation is excessively fragmented and conspicuously underdeveloped, with no really large companies yet.

It's not that consumers don't want better cemeteries and services. The demand is there. And it's not that the companies aren't competing to provide the supply. Companies are trying to grow in both scale and services, similar to Operational Marathon. But in this case, they are mostly running on a treadmill. They are running really hard but nobody is getting anywhere. Fu Shou Yuan has annual revenue of about $100M after 20 years of operations. Chinese real estate developers can make more than that with a couple of projects.

Deathcare is a good example of a competitive situation we call the Treadmill. This is in the bottom right of the China Consumer Pyramid, where there is no competitive advantage and the State is an active force against what you are doing. This is one place you really don't want to be in China. Not only is there endless competition but the State doesn't really want you to succeed. For whatever reason, the State doesn't want the industry to develop or change or take off. Or it doesn't want your type of company to succeed. You don't really fail in a Treadmill. You just never win. You work hard for years, sometimes decades, and never get very far.

The Treadmill
(photo by Pressmaster/Shutterstock)

When new China opportunities like deathcare are point-ed to with great enthusiasm and proclaimed to be inev-itable, a good question is always, "Well, if it is so great then why hasn't it happened yet?" If something hasn't happened yet, there are probably good reasons why. Our advice is that life is short and China is big. Recognize a Treadmill as a no-win situation and focus your time else-where.

We consider Treadmills a specific situation in a larger cat-egory we call the State Carnival. According to our China Consumer Pyramid, this is the bottom right where there is no competitive advantage and the State is an active force. But the State Carnival actually has lots of different games you can play. Some are difficult (like Treadmills). Some are really great. And many are just sort of chaotic and nonsensical. What they all have in common is that the economics are fundamentally political. Some games have logical economics. Some games are just the result of self-interests and rules that have accumulated over time.

Some games at the State Carnival can be pretty attractive. In some cases, the State is active in supporting an indus-try's development, or a particular type of company. Usu-ally that means providing a lot of cheap credit. We have seen this game in solar energy, real estate and healthcare. It usually works quite well short term and can rapidly accelerate an industry's development. However, there is often a painful correction in the long term.

The State Carnival
(photo by Matthew Cole/Shutterstock)

Our point is, if you are at the State Carnival, know you have a ton of competition and you are living in politically created economics.

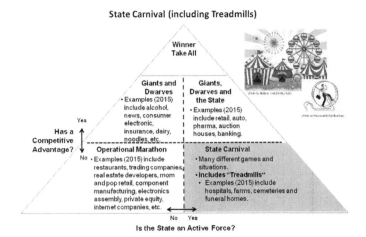

For those who want to know more about this, please refer to the flow chart below. or the Appendix.

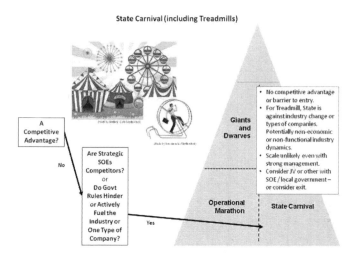

IS THE FUNERAL INDUSTRY FINALLY AT A TAKE-OFF POINT?

"Take-off points" are important in China. These are the points when most people become wealthy enough to comfortably afford a product. You can see in the chart below that when the majority of people reach these points spending accelerates quickly. And it is important to note these points don't happen at the same time for every product, even within a product category (refrigerators vs. washing machines shown below).

Take-off points and accelerations vary by product

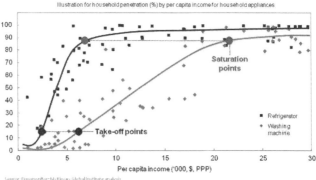

Illustration for household penetration (%) by per capita income for household appliances

Per capita income ('000, $, PPP)

Source: Euromonitor; McKinsey Global Institute analysis

So are we going to see a take-off in deathcare? In this case, it is about the government's intentions and interests. As we are writing this, the government is working on a funeral and interment reform. This will likely include a ban on expensive burials but it may open up the sector as well. And keep in mind, the State still owns the majority of the cemeteries and burial sites nationwide (State-Related Assets is one of our five government impacts). The Ministry of Civil Affairs' green paper on funerals noted there were 3,754 units in funeral services at the end of 2008, among them 1,692 funeral homes, 1,209 cemeteries governed by the Ministry of Civil affairs and 853 units of funeral management. So the State is deeply involved by regulations, by companies and by assets. Apart from the State, the other players in this sector are mostly small-to-medium family-owned enterprises.

The hope of many is that we are finally witnessing a take-off point in the industry. There is public criticism of the sales techniques and obscure pricing used by many companies in the funeral industry. The upcoming regulations could bring structural changes, including the participation of more operators and more transparent pricing. This is a State-controlled industry and the State appears to be preparing to restructure it.

How could the sector develop? This is where Jonathan engages with his strategy thinking. And Jeff defaults to his standard "always go with what is proven" value investor mantra.

Jeff's answer to this question is:

- In China, it is better to follow proven economics, such as real estate and consumer spending. Don't wait for new sources of revenue to emerge from the ether. Look at where the big money is already moving, piggy-back that and focus on eliminating your competition.

- For deathcare, that means following a quasi real-estate strategy. Real estate is a big and proven economic engine. Buy land and do real estate development. Or buy and sell plots. Services can complement this but the proven, big economic engine is real estate.

- Don't go chasing attractive demographics with unproven economics.

Jonathan's answer is:

- There is usually a good reason for things to be the way they are. The funeral services business is a very local one. People take dying seriously and want to have confidence in their local undertaker.

- The only way to scale up is to have the margins to support local services while undercutting mom-and-pop businesses. This translates into being able to offer something pretty unique, which is probably ultimately going to be real estate related.

FINAL POINT: LARGE SECTIONS OF THE CHINESE ECONOMY WILL NEVER BE RATIONAL OR RATIONALIZED

China's middle class is an obsession for a lot of analysts, economists and government officials. It is big and growing fast. And not to be morbid (too late), but what goes up must one day come down. So taking care of bodies could generate a lot of business.

However, elderly consumers are not yet the attractive demographic everyone thinks they are. Consumer products, adult education, tourism and many other elderly-focused businesses have largely not taken off. And in the case of deathcare, you have the additional problem that it has been stuck on the Treadmill for 30 years. If you are betting on such things changing this year, you will probably be disappointed.

Generally people get sucked into bad industries because of compelling demographics or because they expect the industry to be rational. The result is usually not failure.

The result is wasted years, and sometimes decades. Our advice is don't get lured in by attractive consumer demographics. And keep in mind, certain segments of the Chinese economy are not rational and will not be rationalized any time soon. The government has the cash to support non-economic behavior in some areas and is often prepared to do so for a long time.

A typical Chinese cemetery
(photo by yojik / Shutterstock)

CHAPTER #5:
HOW THE NBA CONVINCED A BILLION CHINESE TO CARE ABOUT BASKETBALL

The game of basketball is not new to China. It came to the Mainland shortly after Canadian-American James Naismith invented it in Massachusetts in 1891. A local chapter of the Young Men's Christian Association likely organized the first basketball game in China in March of 1896. The sport subsequently spread somewhat and is reported to have even been played by soldiers during the Long March.

Soccer actually has a much longer history in China and the sport may have originated there. FIFA claims that the earliest competitive form of soccer was an exercise practiced by the Han dynasty military called Tsu Chu. In that game, two teams kicked a leather ball filled with feathers and hair through a 1,600-square-cm opening with a net. Players could move the ball with their feet, shoulders and chests but the use of hands was not permitted. English rules for the sport were introduced in the early 19th century. A young Mao Zedong even played goalkeeper at his teacher's college.

We can conclude two things from these histories. First, basketball and soccer (and many other Western sports) were introduced to China a long time ago. And second, none of them gained much widespread adoption. Neither basketball, football, soccer nor baseball were widely played or even watched in China even 30 years ago.

So how do you explain the following facts about the NBA in China today?

- China is the #1 international market for the NBA.

- Four to five NBA games are broadcast on State television weekly.

- Typically viewership of weekly games is +30M.

- During important NBA games, Chinese viewership can reach 200M.

- The NBA's official China blog has 27.5M fans.

- There are 70M NBA followers on various Chinese social media.

- Chinese President Xi Jinping says he enjoys watching NBA games in his spare time.

The key question for this chapter is: **How did the NBA convince so many Chinese to suddenly care about basketball?** How did that happen? And why didn't it happen for other sports? A question the NFL and MLB have no doubt asked.

The common answer to this question is the superstardom of Chinese basketball player Yao Ming. But this is, at best, only part of the answer. We argue that the NBA's conspicuous success in China is mostly the result of clever business strategy by former NBA Commissioner David Stern.

This final story also includes our last group of Chinese consumers, 15- to 24-year-old Chinese who are currently entering the workforce. A few key points about this important group.

While it is often reported that 300M Chinese play basketball, this is doubtful. However, 300M Chinese definitely watch it on television.
(Photo by XiXinXing / Shutterstock)

KEY POINT 1: YOUNG CHINESE ARE THE EMOTIONAL, BIG-SPENDING CONSUMERS THE WORLD HAS BEEN WAITING FOR

There are approximately 200M people between 15 and 24 years of age in China today. They are about 15% of the population and have, by and large, been raised in abundance. Unlike previous generations, most have no memory of hunger or extreme hardship. They have mostly grown up in modern apartments with modern conveniences.

Additionally, the one child policy came into effect in the early 1980's so most of this group is only children. They typically have two parents, four grandparents and no siblings. That does make them the center of attention somewhat, or at least the center of family spending. And they are also more likely to be male. The one child policy has led to a gender skew towards boys.

These young Chinese are the demographic that is most similar to consumers in developed economies. They are more brand loyal than other middle class consumers. They are more interested in trying new products. They are more emotional and less concerned with being frugal. They are willing to trade up rapidly. And they are really confident about their own financial futures (which enables spending).

Basically, this is the demographic the whole world has been waiting for: emotional, confident, big- spending Chinese consumers.

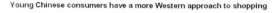

Young Chinese consumers have a more Western approach to shopping

% of Consumer Respondents by Segment

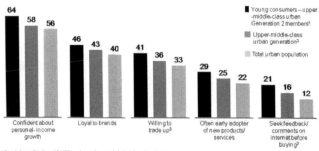

1 People born after the mid-1980s and raised in a period of relative abundance
2 Annual household income of 106,000—229,000 renminbi (equivalent to $16,000 to $34,000 in 2010 real terms)
3 Personal-care-product example

Source: 2012 McKinsey Survey of 10,000 Chinese consumers

Finally, it almost goes without saying that young consumers are a lot more wired. They are overwhelmingly online and 90% have mobile phones. If you want to reach young

Chinese consumers, you need a strategy for smartphones and the Internet.

KEY POINT 2: IN CHINA, IT IS THE YOUNG, NOT THE OLD, WHO HAVE MONEY TO SPEND

As mentioned, in China, it is younger people who are richer and consume more. Young Chinese with jobs are making incomes orders of magnitude higher than their parents did at their age. By 2020, 35% of consumption in China is expected to come from young consumers.

And young Chinese consumers, unsurprisingly, spend their money on somewhat different things. They are major purchasers of leisure, personal services and high-end hospitality. They also spend a lot on travel. The markets for wedding planning, cosmetology and boutique resorts are going through the roof at the moment. And these industries are focusing mostly on people under 30. Additionally, young consumers benefit from total household spending. For example, educational spending by Chinese families has been rising by over 40% annually and this is focused on the kids.

DELAYED COMMITMENTS = MORE SPENDING
In a 2012 McKinsey study, there was some fascinating data on how young Chinese are increasingly delaying certain life events. They are getting married later. They are having children later. This mostly follows from career pressures. But it also follows from higher incomes and different expectations in life.

For example, in 2010 approximately 25% of Chinese high school students went to college. That number is expected to increase to about 40% by 2020. Going to college and then getting a job usually means delaying marriage, family and other commitments. And that is a significant change in the Chinese tradition of marrying in your early twenties, especially for women. In the past 10 years, the average age at which women have children in China has increased from 24 to 27. If this continues, as is expected, it will soon be closer to 30, which is similar to developed countries.

Peking University, where the skies are never this blue. There are now approximately 8M Chinese college graduates per year.
(photo by hidear / Shutterstock)

Another consequence of this delaying of life events is greater spending. Young people who stay single longer have more time and money. This means more hobbies, more vacations, nicer apartments and so on. And this also eventually leads to more expensive weddings (and divorces).

This delaying of commitments means women in particular have more money. A 2012 McKinsey study found that women's participation in the China workforce is now at 67%, way above the 33% in India and the 58% in the USA. Additionally, Chinese women are more financially ambitious than women in most other countries. One study found that 76% of women in China are aiming for top jobs in their companies, compared with 52% in the USA. They have more to spend before they marry and they often become the primary financial decision-makers after marriage.

Young women and working moms are an incredibly important consumer demographic.
(photo by wong sze yuen/Shutterstock)

KEY POINT 3: CHINESE CONSUMERS REALLY, REALLY LOVE SPORTS

We have discussed various intersections of consumers, competition and government. But in each case, the consumer factor was almost a given. Chinese consumers were already buying beer and food. And buying Chinese art was not a stretch. But in this case, the consumer factor (watching basketball) is far more speculative.

According to the Gemba Group, approximately 60% of Chinese regularly watch sports on CCTV. In addition, about 53% said they watch sports via cable. And 32% say they watch online. So starting with 1.3 billion Chinese, it turns out there is a pretty huge population of sports viewers in China.

It also turns out that Chinese are more enthusiastic about sports than people in most other countries. A YouGov survey of +21,000 people in 15 international markets found that 30% of Chinese are "very passionate" about soccer. That was the highest response of any country. The global average for "very passionate" fans was 17%. And only 10% in the United Kingdom. Even Argentina and Spain were less at 27% and 26%. Of course, in Chinese soccer there is also the quirk that fans overwhelmingly prefer any team to their national team (only 25% of Chinese fans root for their home team during a soccer match).

That survey was for soccer but it is safe to assume that it probably applies to basketball as well. Young consumers and sports fans are critical demographics for the NBA in China. And it turns out they really do like sports.

There are also some interesting studies on Chinese sports fans and "logic of mastery" types of fanship. These types of fans tend to focus more on the history of the sport, on the players, on the statistics and on the team strategies. It is an intellectual mode of engagement, as opposed to fanship based on pride, social connection, play or identification. This seems to be a big factor in China. As a result, Chinese sports fans are the most likely to read about the sport and listen to postgame recaps.

***

THE AWESOME STORY OF DAVID STERN AND THE NBA IN CHINA

This story begins in 1978-9 with two important events. First, Abe Pollin, owner of the then champion Washington Bullets, received an invitation from Deng Xiaoping to come to China. While both China and the US had exchanged amateur athletic delegations prior, the Washington Bullets' visit to China was the first time a professional North American team had visited the newly opened China.

Second, the NBA's long-time outside lawyer David Stern joined the company as General Counsel. A New York City native, David had attended Rutgers University and Columbia Law School prior to becoming a lawyer at Proskauer Rose in 1966. And he had been an outside lawyer for the NBA since almost the day he graduated law school. By the time he joined the NBA as General Counsel in 1978 (and also became Executive Vice President) he had worked with the NBA for 12 years. And within 5 years of joining, he had succeeded Larry O'Brien as commissioner.

David ended up being the NBA commissioner for 30 years. And during that period, he turned the NBA into a global sports powerhouse. But his success in China is arguably his most impressive. And his first major move in the PRC happened in 1987.

In 1987, the NBA went to China and struck a deal with Chinese State television provider CCTV. The deal was that the NBA would send videotapes with game footage for CCTV to broadcast. And they would divide the advertising revenue from these broadcasts (which was negligible at that time). These NBA highlights tapes were sent weekly from New York and began to make basketball free to watch across much of China. Beginning in 1987, Chinese viewers began to be introduced to the NBA and to players like Magic Johnson and Larry Bird.

There was also some good luck early on. The same year David Stern became commissioner, Michael Jordan and Charles Barkley both joined the league. Additionally, the Chicago Bulls then arrived and became a global phenomenon. And in 1992, basketball appeared in the Olympics (which has big China viewership) and the world was introduced to the American "dream team". By the early 1990's, the CCTV-NBA viewership and advertising revenues had began to grow. And soon NBA games were being shown by province- and city-level broadcasters as well as by CCTV.

The strategy the NBA pursued in China was one of free mass dissemination. David Shoemaker, CEO of NBA China, later stated, "It's been very important for the NBA since we started in the 1980's to make our games accessible to as broad an audience as possible." However, free dissemination meant revenue would have to come from advertisements or some other source. It also required successfully partnering with CCTV, a strategic and sometimes bureaucratic Chinese SOE. So it sounds logical but it is not as easy as it seems. It is worth taking a moment to compare the NBA's approach with that of the English Premier League (EPL).

As mentioned, soccer also has a long history in China. Similar to basketball, there was some level of baseline interest, if not enthusiasm, for the sport. And for many years, the EPL had a similar content partnership with CCTV. But the model they use in most foreign countries is actually pay-per-view. This customer-pays-for-content arrangement limits their viewership, especially in poorer countries. But it allows the EPL to attract viewers with higher incomes. It attracts more passionate viewers. And, most importantly, it means cash up front from the local broadcast partner. That helps the soccer teams purchase top players. And it reflects that fact that the soccer teams operate relatively independently in terms of money, with the EPL more of an umbrella organization. EPL's total broadcast agreements are worth approximately $2.5B per year, with about half of that coming from overseas rights.

In 2007, the EPL signed a pay-per-view agreement with Chinese WinTV, ending the free availability of EPL through CCTV. It was reported that WinTV, run by State-owned Guangdong Provincial Television, won the EPL rights with an offer of $50M for three seasons.

The results were disastrous. The Guardian reported that EPL's viewership in China dropped from 30M to approximately 20,000 following the move to pay-per-view. And within the first year, the WinTV yearly subscription price for EPL was reportedly cut from $250 to $77. The move misjudged the Chinese consumer's willingness to pay. It also misjudged the role of strategic SOEs in China's media landscape. CCTV is still one of the few major licensed Mainland television broadcasters.

In contrast, the NBA has continued their long partnership with CCTV. For the recent NBA finals in the US, CCTV sent over 50 journalists to cover the two-week series. No other country sent a group even half that size. Further, the NBA's deal with CCTV has increased over the years and now includes broadcasts on seven of CCTV's regional radio and television providers.

And within all this, the NBA has retained their intellectual property. According to Joseph Ravitch of the Raine Group, "The key to that deal is that NBA China owns all of the rights, past, present and future, to all NBA trademarks, all NBA content, all the video past, present and future, for greater China."

So if we were writing this in 2001, we would say that the NBA in China was in a Giants, Dwarves and the State situation. By virtue of a successful partnership with CCTV, one of the few broadcast channels available at that time, the NBA had become one of the major sports entertainment companies in China. Was this because Chinese viewers really liked basketball? Yes. Was it because of Michael Jordan? Probably. Or was it because it was one of the few things on when State TV was dominant? Definitely.

YAO MING LAUNCHES THE NBA CHINA INTO THE STRATOSPHERE

You can make an analogy between Chinese watching basketball in the 1990's and Americans watching The Ed Sullivan Show in the 1960's. Americans weren't watching because Ed Sullivan was particularly great looking. In fact, he was a pretty ugly guy to be on television. Most Americans watched him because there were only three television stations back then and he was what was on.

And then one day in 1964, the Beatles appeared on The Ed Sullivan Show. And Americans went crazy. A powerful competitive dynamic was overwhelmed by a consumer and cultural phenomenon.

We argue that the early success of the NBA in China was similar. Their early success was due to mass dissemination of popular content plus this same Ed Sullivan-type competitive dynamic. People liked it. But it was also one of the few things on television at that time. And this built up a consumer base over many years.

If the NBA-CCTV deal was The Ed Sullivan Show, then Yao Ming was the Beatles. He showed up on the stage one day and the Chinese went crazy. It was a cultural phenomenon. Within a few years, he was leading the Chinese team in the Beijing Olympics' Opening Ceremony, figuratively and literally carrying the Chinese flag.

Yao was already somewhat famous in China prior to the NBA. His mother and father had both played basketball professionally. Yao had been successful in the Chinese Basketball Association. And he was known for being crazy tall. By his 10th birthday, he was already six feet tall. Plus, he was an extremely relatable person. He had succeeded through the State-sponsored athletic system, an opportunity available to any Chinese citizen. Plus, the Chinese just liked him. And when he joined the NBA in 2002, they went crazy.

According to New York University Professor Luis Cabral, in the years after Yao joined the Houston Rockets, a game was normally viewed by 1M people in the US would attract up to 30M viewers in China. In Yao's first season, the NBA signed contracts with 12 local Chinese TV stations, doubling the number of games broadcast to 170.

Yao was a consumer phenomenon. But he also greatly benefitted from the consumer base that had been built in the 1990's. Houston Rockets games had already been watched on CCTV for years. The NBA already had a Chinese language website. And NBA stars had already been touring China in the off seasons.

The Yao phenomenon peaked during the 2008 Summer Olympics, where he was effectively master of ceremonies. He has since retired and people tend to point to him as the obvious reason for the NBA's success in China. But they forget that CCTV has now been broadcasting NBA games in China for 27 years. Yao was critical but so were the periods prior to and after his involvement.

POST-YAO, RISING CHINESE CONSUMERS KEEP LIFTING THE NBA

In February 2011, New York Knicks star Jeremy Lin created another Yao-like surge of interest in basketball. While "Linsanity" helped boost the NBA's China momentum, it also raised questions about the NBA China post-Yao. Without a relatable figure for China to rally around, would maintaining interest and viewership be difficult?

The answers appears to be no. The reality is that post-Yao, the NBA is more popular than ever in China. There are lots of explanations floating around for this. Some argue that the sport is now mostly a consumer phenomenon and has always benefitted from its long history in China (factory workers used to play basketball for fitness). Some argue the sport is uniquely suited to an urban environment. Some argue that soccer and other sports have had poor management (and some scandals). Some claim basketball is somewhat similar to tai chi and the focus on movement resonates. Some claim it is because Michael Jordan and Yao Ming both were on teams that happened to wear red uniforms.

Our explanation is that David Stern effectively managed an evolving mix of consumer, competitive and government factors. The NBA succeeded initially because of the enthusiasm of Chinese consumers and because it captured a Giants, Dwarves and the State situation (i.e., the CCTV partnership). And then Yao Ming, a consumer phenomenon, came along and that further rocketed them upwards. However, since then things have actually gotten even better. By virtue of some particularly clever strategic moves, the NBA has become a unique China business with virtually no competition.

THE NBA CHINA BECOMES A UNIQUE AND POWERFUL CROSS-BORDER MEDIA PLATFORM

By 2004-2005, the NBA China plus Yao Ming had begun to occupy a unique media position between the US and China. Western brands discovered they could reach millions of Chinese through the NBA. Similarly, Chinese companies seeking to go global found they could advertise at NBA games and reach both Western and Chinese audiences at the same time. And even domestically focused Chinese companies found that they could reach Chinese consumers by advertising at games in the US. For example, Yanjing Beer began buying courtside advertising at NBA games in Houston, even though their products were not being sold in the USA. The NBA became almost an entirely unique US-China advertising platform.

Lots of big companies became deeply invested in the success of the NBA in China. For example, the 2004 China Games exhibition tour was sponsored by Coca-Cola, Anheuser-Busch, Nike, Disney and McDonald's. They sponsored the tour and advertised at the games. But they also supported the NBA at their own China businesses. Customers at Chinese McDonald's outlets received NBA posters with their meals. Nike provided uniforms to the China High School Basketball League. And Coca-Cola hosted an NBA Jam Tour with basketball clinics and parties with NBA stars. Virtually everyone was pushing for the NBA China to be successful. Yao Ming commented at the time, "We can use the NBA to promote the China market . . . The [sponsors] are helping me and I am helping them. It's mutually beneficial."

The list of Chinese sponsors for the NBA has since grown and many of China's largest companies, including Tencent, Lenovo, Peak, Dongfeng, and Haier, now align themselves with the NBA. This continues to fuel their unique cross-border position.

These strategic moves have effectively eliminated the competition for the NBA in China. Replicating what they have done – dedicated viewership by enthusiastic Chinese consumers, the world's only basketball league, a unique US-China media platform – is probably now impossible.

On February 1, 2014, David Stern stepped down as commissioner, exactly 30 years to the day after he began. He was the longest-serving commissioner in NBA history. And during his tenure, he increased revenue over 30-fold, launched seven new franchises and turned the league into a global phenomenon. Today, the NBA has 12 offices outside the US and its games are seen in 215 countries. And to answer our initial question, he is the person who got a billion Chinese to care about basketball.

NBA Commissioner David Stern at a press conference for the 2012 NBA China Games in Shanghai
(Photo by ImagineChina)

KEY POINT 4: THE NBA CHINA IS NOW A "WINNER TAKE ALL" SITUATION

Our China Consumer Pyramid has five situations based on various combinations of consumers, competition and State involvement. Some of these situations are daunting and Darwinian, such as Operational Marathons. Some are great and lucrative, such as Giants, Dwarves and the State. But what every company hopes for is a "Winner Take All" position at the top of the pyramid. And that is what the NBA China has achieved.

Winner Take All means you have both a competitive advantage and dominant market share. There are no other Giants and you are protected from new entrants. It's not a monopoly but it can be pretty close to it. That means you have good, and sometimes great, profit margins. And you usually have attractive returns on capital (ROIC-WACC). To be riding the current wave of Chinese consumer spending without competitors is about as good as it gets in business. Life is great at the top of the pyramid.

In the US, there are a few big Winner Take All companies like Facebook and Google. However, such dominance nationally is actually quite rare. And you almost never see this internationally. It's simply too hard to have such dominance and exclusivity over such big geographies. These situations are far more common at the local or regional level, such as a really dominant furniture store in Omaha, the only granite quarry in a small town or the only restaurant in an airport terminal.

Winner Take All
(Photo by Robert Adrian Hillman/Shutterstock)

How you define the market is important. You can see such dominance in specific functions, customer segments or geography. Generally small, local service companies are the most common Winner Take All situations.

Winner Take All

Winner Take All
• Includes strategic SOEs, Internet Co, local services, etc.

Giants and Dwarves
• Examples (2015) include alcohol, news, consumer electronic, insurance, dairy, noodles, etc.

Giants, Dwarves and The State
• Examples (2015) include retail, auto, pharma, auction houses, banking.

Has a Competitive Advantage?

Yes

No

Operational Marathon
• Examples (2015) include restaurants, trading companies, real estate developers, mom and pop retail, component manufacturing, electronics assembly, private equity, internet companies, etc.

State Carnival
• Many different games and situations.
• Includes "Treadmills"
  • Examples (2015) include hospitals, farms, cemeteries and funeral homes.

No   Yes
Is the State an Active Force?

In China, a Winner Take All position almost always requires good State relationships. Of course, if the company is the largest furniture business in Kunming, government relations are a necessary but not critical issue. However, if the sector is Internet search (e.g., Baidu), e-commerce (e.g., Alibaba), telecommunications (e.g., China Mobile) or media (e.g., the NBA), then good relationships with the government are critical for management. Basically, engage with the regulator before he engages with you.

The NBA China has achieved something close to a Winner Take All position. There are certainly lots of other sports one can watch. And there are tons of entertainment options. But the NBA China has such a powerful position in the brains of Chinese consumers that there are simply no other serious basketball leagues as competitors. Chinese consumers love basketball and the NBA is basketball. Additionally, they have a unique US-China media platform, something no other sport or league has built. As mentioned, this sort of dominance depends on how you define the market – by geography, function, customer-type, strategic group, etc.

Let us add a final caveat. We have basically presented a model for several common China phenomena. However, no model fits real-world situations perfectly. Per Nobel laureate Richard Feynman, "Every theoretical physicist who is any good knows six or seven different theoretical representations for exactly the same physics." We have presented one model. But you really want to have multiple models for the same business phenomena.

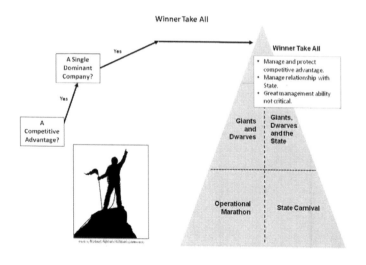

A FINAL QUESTION: HOW DO YOU GO FROM BIG BASKETBALL VIEWERSHIP TO BIG PARTICIPATION?

The biggest problem for the NBA in China today is that people are watching but not actually playing. Or at least not very much. Despite dubious claims about 300M Chinese playing basketball, viewership dwarfs actual participation. And discussions about participation tend to jump quickly to discussions about real estate projects. The idea is that if you build the courts, people will start to play. This argument also syncs nicely with the national obsession with real estate.

As a result, we are now seeing lots of basketball infrastructure being built in China. The country has committed to building approximately 800,000 basketball courts. This is about basketball but it is also about developing more livable cities. For example, Southern Zhuhai has a plan for 150 basketball courts downtown, but this is mostly to provide a little bit of green space for the community.

The crown jewel of the current basketball infrastructure push is 12 big arenas to be built across China. Local governments are going to provide the financing, but the development will be done by a joint venture between the NBA and AEG. Additionally, the NBA is planning a 120,000-square-foot basketball and entertainment complex outside of Beijing.

This is all pretty logical and seems likely to succeed. And, as we saw at the 2008 Olympics, if you can combine two national obsessions (sports and real estate), things happen pretty fast in China.

Beijing after the 2008 Olympics.
(photo by Sean Pavone / Shutterstock)

FINAL POINT: YOU CAN HAVE A PRIVATE MONOPOLY IN STATE CAPITALISM

The NBA in China is an impressive story and highlights an important point: You can win it all in China. You can have a private monopoly in State capitalism. And then you just sit back and enjoy as Chinese consumers become wealthier and wealthier. But your business had better be a world-class proposition.

Looking back, many of the things that made the NBA so successful in China have now changed. Dominant State media channels have given way to online streaming and content available virtually everywhere. CCTV, in particular, is losing influence as more Chinese watch online.

The NBA has gone online and is doubling down on its mass-diffusion China strategy. In January 2015, they announced a new exclusive digital partnership with fellow Winner Take All company Tencent. Through its various portals (QQ.com, QQ, Qzone, Weixin, etc.), Tencent reaches hundreds of millions of Chinese PC and mobile phone users on a daily basis. This new partnership with the NBA will live-stream NBA games (including All-Star Games, Playoffs and Finals) through most of Tencent's channels. The NBA also has a partnership with Tencent to deliver the official NBA 2K mobile game. As of 2014, NBA 2K Online had 19M registered accounts and is the #1 PC online sports game in China.

The days of Chinese consumers not having access to much content are long gone. It is now a free-for-all for Chinese eyeballs, particularly the online and big-spending younger consumers. For the NBA, nailing this new digital environment will be as crucial as the TV strategy of the last decades.

The next generation of sports media in China will be an entirely new world.
(photo by Fabio Fantuzzi / Shutterstock)

CONCLUSION: CHINA HAS A GREAT F@*$#G MACRO- CONSUMER STORY

On a fairly regular basis, Jeff goes off on a rant in these books (usually about what he considers bad modeling). Jonathan then quietly deletes it. In a refreshing twist, the below is a rare Jonathan rant. So we are definitely keeping it in.

The rant is this. China has an awesome macro consumer story. It hasn't always been that way but for sure it's that way now. And it's getting really tiring listening to continual moaning about slowing growth and the need for rebalancing. We have three main points on this.

#1 - DON'T WORRY ABOUT CONSUMER SPENDING AS A PERCENTAGE OF GDP.

Like most developing Asian economies, China's early growth was based on investment and exports. You get your population to move to the cities, work in factories and make stuff. This is exported and cash is brought back home for investment. Plus you get some foreign investment as well. This process enabled China to develop its infrastructure largely with its own cash. That, by the way, is not the norm. Developing economies typically borrow from foreigners and then default. For example, American states like Mississippi and Florida were chronic defaulters on foreign debt as they initially developed.

One of the downsides of this investment-first approach is that it makes consumption look small and often like it's shrinking. Chinese consumption has decreased from approximately 51% of GDP in 1985 to 44% in 1995 and to 38% in 2005. And then it went down to 34% in 2013. This is in comparison to consumption in Japan at 57% and the US at about 70%. China's small and decreasing consumption percentage is one reason why people keep talking about "rebalancing" (i.e., the need for more consumer spending relative to investment and net exports).

Our position is don't worry about this stuff:

- First, from 2000 to 2010, the size of the Chinese economy more than tripled. So consumption grew from around $550M (RMB 4.6T) to $2T (RMB 13.7T). Regardless of the relative percent of GDP, China's consumption has been growing faster than just about any other country in absolute terms.

- Second, just getting consumer spending back to 44% of GDP, the level in 1995, would have a huge impact on "rebalancing". It would also create the largest consumer market in the world.

- Third, most of these numbers are wildly inaccurate. Consumer spending is nearly impossible to measure in such a big, complicated economy. Combining that vague number with two other big vague numbers (investment and net exports) is very fuzzy math. Until economists start putting uncertainty estimates on their China calculations, relative percentages aren't worth paying much attention to.

#2 - HOUSEHOLD INCOME IS WHAT YOU REALLY CARE ABOUT. AND IT'S GREAT.

The number you really want to keep in mind is household income. You can't have consumption without income. And here's where it gets really awesome. China's household income is huge. It is now likely above $5T per year. Plus lots of income is unreported, so this is really the lower bound for true household income.

Developing economies, especially the BRICs, are frequently grouped together but Chinese consumers dwarf all the other groups in terms of household income. Note the below chart.

China's household income dwarfs other emerging markets

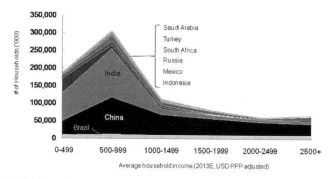

Source: Credit Suisse emerging consumer survey, World Bank Databook.

#3 - RISING DISCRETIONARY SPENDING IS THE EXCITING PART.

Discretionary spending is the stuff you like but don't need. Or you only sort of need. And fortunately people seem to have an endless appetite for this (entertainment, skiing, lattes, etc.).

Chinese citizens are now moving beyond being able to only afford the basics of life and their discretionary spending is taking off. Growth in annual discretionary categories in China is estimated at +7% percent between 2010 and 2020. There is also a second category of "semi-necessities", which is expected to grow at about 6-7%. And both of these categories are growing faster than spending on necessities, which are expected to grow around 5% (about the same as expected GDP growth).

Discretionary categories are showing the fastest growth

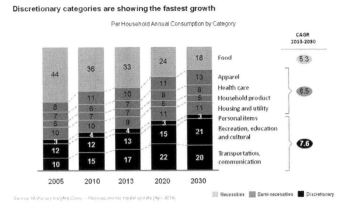

Per Household Annual Consumption by Category

An important related issue is the Chinese tradition of saving. Note the below chart on spending vs. saving across the emerging markets. The spike in Chinese savings is fairly understandable. First, it's cultural. Second, they are precautionary savings. No social safety net means if you get sick it's all on you. Third, Chinese savings are not so unique. Japan, Taiwan and Korea all hit a 30%-plus savings rate in their early development. And fourth, if there isn't much of a consumer finance system it's challenging to leverage yourself up to truly spectacular consumption levels – like buying vacation homes or cars that cost as much as your annual income.

That's our rant on China's macro consumer situation. Basically it's a great story. It is volatile. It is somewhat unpredictable. But you just don't get a consumer growth story this good anywhere else. We are now going to retreat back to the micro level where we belong.

Spending versus saving in China and other emerging markets (% monthly)

Source: Credit Suisse Emerging Consumer Survey

A FINAL MICRO STORY

In May 2014, a group of Chinese tourists took a one-week organized trip to Los Angeles. They flew from China, stayed in hotels and traveled around seeing the sights in tour buses. What was interesting about this particular tour group was that it had over 7,000 people. They boarded 86 planes in China, occupied 26 hotels in Los Angeles and traveled around in 160 buses. They also apparently had some fun descending on various locations en masse.

That is a good final story for Chinese consumers and their increasing impact on the world. Because who saw a 7,000-person tour group coming? Not only is this a big economic phenomenon but so much of it is unpredictable.

Another example: Over 30M Chinese live in caves. This is mostly in Shaanxi province and they are a larger population than Saudi Arabia or Scandinavia. We're not really sure what to think about that.

THE GAMEBOARD IS DYNAMIC

As we said in the Introduction, there are two views of China intertwined here. The first is the consumer story, which is inspiring but also far more complicated that commonly assumed. A huge number of people are moving from subsistence living to having their own homes, cars, washing machines, and college diplomas. This transition will only happen once and it may end up being the most important event of our time. Plus it's a lot of fun. Can you imagine 160 buses of Chinese tourists passing you on the freeway?

The other view is the ruthless fight for these consumers. Most companies fail to survive in this market, let alone win. It's gruesome entertainment. And throughout all of this you have the active involvement of the Chinese government.

We have argued that the most important questions are about competitive advantage and the role of the State. That gets you our China Consumer Pyramid and the five competitive situations we have outlined. Some are great and immensely profitable. Some are absolutely brutal.

Winner Take All. David Stern and the NBA China are a great example of this type of spectacular success. Today, the lucky companies at the top of the pyramid include strategic SOEs, Internet companies like Baidu, Alibaba and Tencent, unique multinationals like the NBA and lots of small and regional companies.

Giants and Dwarves. The regional success of Sunny Wong and Carlsberg is a far more common situation. This is also the good life in China (assuming you are a Giant). These situations today include beer, consumer electronics, insurance, consumer products and several others.

Giants, Dwarves and the State. This is a fairly common and profitable situation in Chinese State capitalism. It includes auction houses like Poly and Guardian, pharmaceuticals, car companies, banks and many others. And it is especially common in industrial and B2B companies. This is a politicized market so if you can't be a Giant (or the State), you probably want to be very helpful to them. For example, be an advanced auto-parts supplier to a State-owned automaker.

Operational Marathon. Unfortunately, this is most business in China. And it is brutal and Darwinian. The great success of Sam Su and KFC was the result of +20 years of hard work against a sea of very hard-working competitors. If you are in this situation, be mentally and financially prepared for the long haul. Examples today are restaurants, small manufacturers, real estate developers and professional service companies. Life in China can be particularly ruthless at the bottom of the pyramid.

State Carnival (and Treadmills). There are lots of interesting games at the State Carnival, usually based on politically created economics. Some games are great, many are mostly confused and some are particularly difficult (Treadmills). Examples of Treadmills today are public hospitals (could be changing), funeral homes, rehabilitation centers and many others. Don't waste your time trying to get ahead in situations that are just too hard.

And finally, be ready for the situation to change. The gameboard in China is dynamic. Consumers can be unpredictable as we mentioned. But the competitive dynamic can also change. For example, Treadmills can become Operational Marathons (e.g., deathcare with new regulations). Operational Marathons can become Giants and Dwarves (e.g., consolidation? Increasing focus on branded food products?). And Giants, Dwarves and the State can become Giants and Dwarves (e.g., privatizations of insurance?). And recall our initial example of the purple Australian Bobbie Bear. That business was clearly going to be an Operational Marathon and they should have anticipated a ton of competitors. But the entry of State then turned it into a Treadmill. And so on.

Our position on all of this is simple:

Point 1: China is now the world's most complicated consumer market. You have to look at it sub-group by sub-group.

Point 2: The importance of China's rising consumers is matched only by the brutality of the fight for them. Most companies fail. Be wary.

Point 3: The State ultimately creates most of the winners. China is still State capitalism and, even in consumer markets, the government is still determining most of the winners.

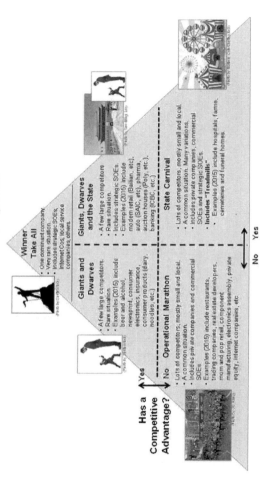

China Consumer Pyramid

Winner Take All
- One dominant company.
- Very rare situation.
- Includes strategic SOEs, Internet Cos, local service companies, others.

Giants, Dwarves and the State
- A few large competitors.
- Rare situation.
- Includes strategic SOEs.
- Examples (2015) include modern retail (Bailian, etc), auto (SAIC, etc), pharma, auction houses (Poly, etc.), banking (ICBC, etc.)

Giants and Dwarves
- A few large competitors.
- Rare situation.
- Examples (2015) include newsprint, consumer electronics, insurance, consumer products (dairy, beer and alcohol, noodles, etc).

State Carnival
- Lots of competitors, mostly small and local.
- A common situation. Many variations.
- Includes private companies, commercial SOEs and strategic SOEs.
- Includes "Treadmills".
- Examples (2015) include hospitals, farms, cemeteries and funeral homes.

Operational Marathon
- Lots of competitors, mostly small and local.
- A common situation.
- Includes private companies and commercial SOEs.
- Examples (2015) include restaurants, trading companies, real estate developers, mom and pop retail, component manufacturing, electronics assembly, private equity, internet companies, etc.

Has a Competitive Advantage?
Yes — No

Is the State an Active Force?
No   Yes

- Are strategic (not commercial) SOEs direct competitors?
- Are regulations against industry development or types of companies?
- Are regulations actively fueling the industry or types of companies?
- Are State-related assets or capabilities decisive in competition?

167

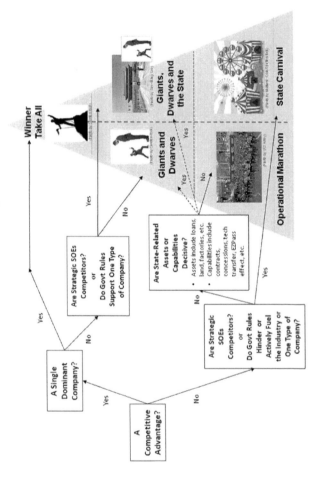

China Consumer Pyramid

A Competitive Advantage?

A Single Dominant Company?

Yes

Are Strategic SOEs Competitors? or Do Govt Rules Support One Type of Company?

No

Are State-Related Assets or Capabilities Decisive?
- Assets include loans, land, factories, etc.
- Capabilities include contracts, concessions, tech transfer, EZPass effect, etc.

No

Are Strategic SOEs Competitors? or Do Govt Rules Hinder or Actively Fuel the Industry or One Type of Company?

Yes

No

Yes

Yes

No

Yes

Winner Take All

Giants and Dwarves

Giants, Dwarves and the State

Operational Marathon

State Carnival

We don't view any of this changing anytime soon. Chinese consumers are going to continue to increase in wealth and complexity. Companies are going to continue to compete and learn to live with communism.

THE MOST IMPORTANT MEGA-TREND IN CHINA IS PEOPLE

The below chart is from our first book. It is the six mega-trends shaping China business. In this chart, we purposefully placed two mega-trends above the line (Rising Chinese Consumers and the Brainpower Behemoth). These two trends are not about factories being built, products being exported or capital being deployed (all of those are below the line). They are not about resources or tangible assets. These two are really about people. Rising consumers and increasing brainpower are where the human elements of the Chinese economy are increasingly playing out.

The 6 China Megatrends

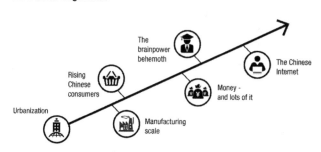

Almost every example in this book has really been about people. About consumers getting wealthier and wiser. About management getting smarter. About competition getting more specialized and sophisticated. About State officials getting more experienced. And so on. As the country develops, these human elements are driving more and more of the economy – and they are the center of China's intertwined consumer, competition and government factors. People tend not to talk about this, mostly because it doesn't really show up in balance sheets or in macroeconomic data. But the intangible human element is really the most important thing going on in China today.

THANKS FOR READING

Thanks for taking the time to read this. If we did our job right, you should be at about 60-80 minutes. Hopefully you feel it was time reasonably well spent.

China is just really big and complicated. You can spend a lifetime struggling with a single part it. And it's getting bigger and more complicated all the time. For example, since 2011 the incremental growth in the Chinese economy has been larger than the entire Indian economy.

Faced with this increasing size and complexity, our approach has been to go small. To focus on common and understandable situations at the micro level. And we have chosen the five small stories in this book carefully. We think you can see these same situations playing out over and over.

We would appreciate any feedback. If you are interested, we have videos on the various chapter topics posted at www.onehourchina.com.

Cheers and thanks,
Jonathan and Jeff

Yalong Bay in Hainan, the "Hawaii of China". It is a pretty nice place for a quick vacation. It is also the site of a major Chinese submarine base. This makes paddling around in the deep water a lot more interesting.
(photo by fuyu liu/Shutterstock)

APPENDIX I:
CHINA CONSUMER PYRAMID SUMMARY

We have detailed five different combinations of consumer, competitive and government factors. In this Appendix, we summarize these situations in a more structured way. We have additional information at the end of Appendix II.

1. OPERATIONAL MARATHON

In Operational Marathon, nobody has a competitive advantage and there are no real barriers to entry. So you are competing against a sea of existing and potential rivals. And in China, that is a huge number of really hard-working people. This should give you serious pause.

China Consumer Pyramid

These industries (sub-industries, strategic groups, etc.) can be concentrated to a few players but most are fragmented with lots of players with small market share. In both cases, profits are usually small and they are characterized by very intense competition. You are basically in a never-ending race against your competitors. And you need to continually develop capabilities, capture operational efficiencies and add operational scale. Hence our name Operational Marathon.

Examples in China in 2015 include restaurants, trading, textiles, toys, residential real estate, electronics assembly and many other sectors. China's well-known electronic marts are a good example. In a single five-story building, you can find hundreds of electronics retailers all selling very similar products. The competition is fierce. Everyone works very hard. And nobody makes much money.

In this situation, the State is a typical regulator, not a competitor, and does not have a big preference for who wins. Commercial SOEs may be present but competition is mostly commercial and the government doesn't much care as long as there are no over-riding issues (such as the industry employing a lot of people).

As this is a situation without a competitive advantage, it's all about management and the daily fight for consumers against existing and potential competitors. You might think this is where private and foreign companies should excel in China. However, domestic companies often do better and foreign companies can be taken aback by the rapacity of local Chinese competition. Local competitors will deeply cut price, play loose with suppliers (and the rules), and introduce products at twice the normal rate of Western companies. Those at the front of the pack are usually the ones who ran faster, longer, and for relatively few rewards. If your competitor is willing to work for very little, you need to be willing to eat bitterness yourself.

To win, which is a relative term here, you have to start running early, run fast every day, be very smart, and avoid making big mistakes. And hopefully you build a lead in operational scale and efficiencies over time. In some cases, this can eventually turn into a competitive advantage.

Overall, this is where competition in China is utterly ruthless. Life is very hard at the bottom of the China consumer pyramid.

2. GIANTS AND DWARVES

In Giants and Dwarves, there are real barriers to entry and a few companies (the Giants) usually hold large market share. They are much larger than the other companies (the Dwarves). This usually means healthy profits and sometimes high ROIC, but not always.

The situation is about having a competitive advantage, such as network economics, customer capture or economies of scale. This competitive advantage may or may not be sustainable depending on management performance and the nature of the business.

Examples in China in 2015 include consumer products (such as beer, milk, and noodles) and some insurance companies such as Ping An. These Giants can be private, foreign or local companies. And they can include commercial, not strategic, SOEs.

In this case, the State is a regulator, not a competitor, not an active force, and, by and large, does not have a preference for who wins. It is an overwhelmingly commercial market with a few giant companies dominating. This is typically for particular activities in a value chain, for particular geographies or for particular customer types - not across an industry. In this situation, SOEs operate commercially, without hard State advantages. But they often have State-related assets (factories, loans) or capabilities (approvals, contracts, etc.) that help them and can be important. Private and foreign giants tend to win when purely operational skills matter more.

In terms of management, you have to be smart to get yourself in a giant position. But after that, you are somewhat protected by your competitive advantage. Your profits should track the health of the industry as long as the other giants are not suicidal or economically irrational. The regulator has the unenviable task of managing this giant-dominated competition, which often amounts to deciding how much of what behavior to allow.

Management's primary duties in this situation are to protect the competitive advantage and to keep the Dwarves small. If you have strong customer capture, this is easy. If you are relying on economies of scale, management playing active defense matters. Giants usually need hard-working but not brilliant management. It also helps to have a reputation for fierce retaliation against new entrants. And, very important, you need to manage the relationship with the other Giants. If they fight, everyone can lose.

Overall, this is very profitable place to be. Life can be good in the middle of the pyramid.

3. GIANT, DWARVES AND THE STATE
In Giants, Dwarves and the State, a few companies (the Giants) also hold large market share and are much larger than the other companies in the market (the Dwarves). This usually means healthy profits and returns on invested capital, but not always. The situation is also about having a competitive advantage. This competitive advantage may or may not be sustainable depending on management performance and the nature of the business.

However, in this case, the State has crashed the Giants' and Dwarves' party. Regulations can be extensive and rapidly changing, and can favor certain parties. Local governments can be actively involved. Sometimes there are State assets or companies.

And sometimes the State becomes active as a competitor. These SOEs are usually strategically focused, as opposed to purely commercially focused. All the players then have to figure out how to adapt to the State as a competitor. Usually this means figuring out what the State wants, helping them achieve it and not sacrificing profits in the process. And it is worth remembering that the State usually gets what it wants, given its overwhelming financial and political resources.

Examples in China in 2015 include the auto industry, where the foreign OEMs operate through JVs with state players by law; the banking sector; and pharma, where JVs are rarer but winning players emphasize their commitment to China through research and development investments.

We argue that when the State is an active force it has five potential impacts on competition and industry structure:

1) **Government-granted competitive advantages** (frequently to strategic SOEs).

2) **Direct involvement with strategic SOEs as competitors.**

3) **Regulations / rules for the industry** – this also includes education and information to the public on State preferences.

4) **State-related assets** – such as land, loans, legacy assets (factories, operating platforms, etc.), tax credits, etc.

5) **State-related capabilities** – technology transfer, government approvals, contracts from SOEs, etc.

In terms of management, you have to be smart to get yourself in a Giant position. But after that, you are somewhat protected by your competitive advantage. Your profits should track the health of your industry and the actions of the State.

Savvy managers know that State involvement has pluses as well as minuses. Profits are often higher in industries where there are State players, as they are usually less efficient. Strategic SOEs usually pursue both government and commercial goals. They can be less competitive, although higher costs may require higher prices to stay solvent. If a Giant can support the government goals while carving out their own piece of the market, profits can be very good.

Management's primary duties in this situation are to protect the competitive advantage, to fight off the Dwarves (and new entrants) and to work with the State (usually strategic SOEs, regulators or local governments). Depending on the situation, a joint venture with a strategic SOE or a local government is often the best approach.

Overall, this can be a surprisingly profitable place to be. Life can be very good in State Capitalism.

4. STATE CARNIVAL

The State Carnival is a collection of many different State-designed and State-managed games. There are no competitive advantages and the State is actively involved. This results in a grab-bag of situations, all with mostly political economics, hence the name the State Carnival.

State involvement is often in pursuit of a goal, which could be economic (commercial performance, growth, profits), political (social stability, employment, etc.), or development-related (a new industry, modernization of an existing industry, etc.). Often the goal is not clear or rational and mostly represents the current interests of various stakeholders (status, career, salaries, etc.). In many cases, the situation is just chaotic with lots of rules and systems chaotically accumulated over time.

We argue that when the State is an active force it has five potential impacts on competition and industry structure:

1) **Government-granted competitive advantages** (frequently to strategic SOEs).

2) **Direct involvement with strategic SOEs as competitors.**

3) **Regulations / rules for the industry** – this also includes education and information to the public on State preferences.

4) **State-related assets** – such as land, loans, legacy assets (factories, operating platforms, etc.), tax credits, etc.

5) **State-related capabilities** – technology transfer, government approvals, contracts from SOEs, etc.

State involvement can shape the industry directly (i.e., a granted competitive advantage, mandated JVs) or it can play out over time as significant factors in ongoing competition (i.e., State-related capabilities or assets). It can be positive or negative. And these effects can be applied to the industry uniformly or to specific types of companies (again in a positive or negative way). And changes in these rules and State involvement can change the structure of the industry and competition quickly.

Some games at the State Carnival can be very positive. Such as when the government fuels industry development and growth, usually by providing low interest loans (or cheap land). There are often also government purchasing contracts, tax breaks and other types of financial support. This can result in dramatic and non-economic increases in investment and supply. Modernization can happen quickly but this type of growth and modernization does tend to result in oversupply and a painful correction. An example in 2015 is the current subsidies and government purchases of electric cars.

Most often, businesses at the State Carnival are neither good nor bad. Government involvement is just creating a mix of political and economic rules. This can be limits to entry (which helps you) or price controls (which hurts you). This situation, while complicated, can often be safer than the ruthless competition in Operation Marathon. But it can also be more dysfunctional.

The worst case at the State Carnival is when not only is there no limit to your competitors but the government is also actively against you and / or the industry. We call that situation the Treadmill.

4A. TREADMILLS

The Treadmill is a specific game at the State Carnival. It is one place you really don't want to be in China. And unfortunately there are usually lots of businesses in this situation. In this case, there is also no competitive advantage or barriers to entry. So like in Operational Marathon, you have a ton of hard-working competitors. But in this case, the State is also against you. So we also call this the regulatory zone of pain.

For whatever reasons, the State doesn't want this industry (or you specifically) to change, develop or take-off. Usually this is a policy issue like we see in deathcare, where the government doesn't want scarce urban land used for cemeteries. Or in agriculture, where small family-owned farms are the financial lifeline for lots of families (so no consolidation in parts of agriculture). Sometimes it is for a commercial reason, such as in the cement business where no one can buy local sand and granite deposits because they are all local government-owned. Sometimes there is no reason. It is just how the industry is.

Examples in China in 2015 include public colleges, public hospitals, cemeteries, farms and lots of other small, mostly local companies. Companies in these sectors can be private, foreign or SOEs, but regardless they are almost all small and not growing fast.

This is basically an Operational Marathon where you can run and run but you never really get anywhere (hence the name Treadmill). The trick here is to recognize the situation and then stop investing time, energy or capital into it. Life is short and the financial capacity of China to be irrational in a sector for a long time is big. Your best case outcome is usually to exit through some joint venture or deal with a local government or SOE. The most common outcome is you end up with a small business after lots of work. Even with great, hard-working management you're just not going to get far. The worst case outcome is you waste years or decades of effort and walk away with little to show for it.

Life can be difficult and stagnant at the bottom right of the pyramid.

5. WINNER TAKE ALL
In Winner Take All, a single company has a competitive advantage and dominant market position. It has limited competition and benefits disproportionately from rising Chinese consumer spending. This usually means very large profits and returns on invested capital.

The key to getting in this enviable position is developing a strong competitive advantage, such as a government mandate, network economics, strong customer capture or large economies of scale. This competitive advantage may or may not be sustainable depending on management performance and the nature of the business. This dominant position must also be perceived as being in China's interest. No winning player can afford to antagonize the State.

Examples in China include strategic SOEs such as Sinopec, China Mobile and State Grid; private internet giants such as Tencent, Alibaba and Baidu (prior to 2012); a few unique MNCs such as the NBA and local and functionally specific service companies (usually private). There are few of these dominant companies nationally but geographically the majority are at the regional or local level. Or they focus on niche customers or functional specialties. Winners can be as simple as the only hospital in a small town or the only five-star resort on the beach.

In terms of management, you have to be smart to get yourself in a dominant position. But after that you can often just cruise along, protected by your competitive advantage. Your profits track the health of your industry and super-smart, hard-working management is not really required.

Management's primary duties in this situation are to protect the competitive advantage and to fight off new entrants. And they need to manage the relationship with the State, which is critical. But otherwise this is relaxed and very profitable living.

Life is great at the top of the pyramid.

APPENDIX II: ADDITIONAL THOUGHTS

- FROM THE INTRODUCTION -

THOUGHTS ON COMPETITIVE ADVANTAGE IN DEVELOPING ECONOMY-STATE CAPITALISM

Over the past thirty years, academics like Michael Porter, management consultants like McKinsey and super-investors like Warren Buffett have developed robust frameworks for thinking about competition and competitive advantage. Three common approaches are:

- An industry structure framework (Porter's five forces)

- Competition based on resources and capabilities

- Competitive advantage analysis

And these three different approaches give, more or less, complimentary views of the same phenomena.

Unfortunately, none of these frameworks really help you much in day-to-day China. While they have been extended successfully from Western industries to multinational companies and even to global competition, there are not terribly useful for understanding competition on the ground in developing economies. And they are really not helpful when looking at competition in developing economy-State capitalism (China, Saudi Arabia, etc.).

An industry structure approach (i.e., Porter's five forces) tends to be too complicated to be useful. And most industries are still emerging so long-term economic forces have limited utility. Resource-based competition tends to be useful in the short-term, but not in the long-term. And a competitive advantage approach is frequently thwarted by the uncertainties created by an activist government.

In China, the role of the State is arguably the first or second most important factor shaping competition and industry structure. And it often appears not as an economic force but as a player with objectives, self-interest and multiple lines of implementation. It is arguably more behavioral self-interest than long-term economics. In Western models, the role of the State is typically a sub-factor, an external trend against competition or a vague "catch-all" bucket for stuff we don't know how to predict. For example, in Michael Porter's five forces government is buried within each of the forces. And in value investing, government is viewed as a vague fourth type of competitive advantage or an external factor (usually just regulations). Both of these underestimate the role of the State. And they both are biased towards government as a long-term economic force, and not an active player with self-interests and multiple lines of implementation.

We have put the State as one of the two most important factors (competitive advantage is always first). And we have put forward a detailed framework for how to understand the impact of the State in these situations (presented in subsequent Chapters). We argue that competition and industry structure in developing economy-State capitalism are overwhelmingly determined by two factors:

- **Competitive advantage**

- **The State as an active force**

If Porter has five forces and Buffett has one (competitive advantage), we have two. These two factors should always be looked at first. If you get a good answers to those two questions (our China Consumer Pyramid), you are 80% of the way there. And you can then dig into lots of other factors. But if you can't answer these two questions, then you probably can't get much clarity on the situation ever.

Our China Consumer pyramid is based on how these two factors shape industry structure and competition. They are our horizontal and vertical axes. That gives us five competitive situations which you can frequently see in China today. And we have given each of the situations a name and a picture, to make them easier to remember. And we have a detailed flow chart for figuring out how to answer these two questions.

If you can clearly identify which competitive situation you are in, you also get a good sense of the management performance and behavior that is required. While profitability and return on capital are largely determined by industry structure, individual company returns ultimately depend on management. So in each competitive situation, we have discussed management requirements (both performance and behavior). Competitive advantage and the role of the State determine industry structure, competitive dynamics and overall financial returns. But management performance and behavior determine individual company performance and returns.

A couple of other caveats:

- Much of Western competitive strategy assumes mostly rational entities. The thinking and frameworks assume reasonable management and tend to be overwhelmingly about economic forces in the long-term. In China, that approach can be useful because the long-term evolution of many industries will mirror the evolution in other countries (beer in China will ultimately evolve similar to beer in the US). But in the short and medium term, competition and industry structure are far more chaotic and irrational. Behavior tends to follow more from the interests of the main players, and less from economics. And these players are companies, consumers and the State. So if you start by looking at the self-interests and behaviors of companies (i.e., management) and the State, you will often get a far more accurate and useful picture. In our flow chart, you can see that we have a strong focus on the players and then assume their decisions are a mix of economics and self-interest.

- We talk a lot about dominant versus fragmented markets. And we do imply that large market share is a prerequisite for profits, and hopefully ROIC. However, this is not exactly true and there are lots of examples of small companies in fragmented industries making significant profits. We actually do not define the "market" so this is consistent, if vague. A small operating company (e.g., a car repair station) might actually have significant market share if you define the local city as its market. But the key factor in all of this is competitive advantage. Companies can be big and dominant without a competitive advantage (Operational Marathon). And small companies can sometimes have niche market share with a strong competitive advantage. The market could be a big or small geography, a big or small functional activity or a big or small customer group. Ultimately, a competitive advantage will show up in market share stability, not necessarily in size or market share.

- Finally, we argue that competition and competitive advantage in developing economy-State capitalism is best studied at the micro level. This is a contrast to most China books which tend to be macro and top-down. Our approach has been to identify micro-situations that are common and can be clearly defined. It is important to resist the temptation to combine such micro-situations into one complete uber-strategy. There is no grand unified theory for competition and competitive advantage. At best, one should hope for a list of well understood small situations and to consider them your circle of competence. Our goal is lots of tools and micro-frameworks. Per Nobel Laureate Richard Feynman, "every theoretical physicist who is any good knows six or seven different theoretical representations for exactly the same physics." We want multiple models for competition at the micro and industry level. And the more uncertainty you have in a market, the more models you want.

Ultimately, all of this is to try to answer two or three questions about the fight for Chinese consumers.

- **Is this an attractive industry?** Some are really attractive. Some are incredibly unattractive.

- **Is this an attractive business?** Within an activity, which companies are strong and which are weak?

- **What is going to happen in this situation going forward?** Most analysis is about predicting what is likely going to happen in the near future (say 3-4 years). And these types of mostly qualitative assessments are the starting point for any investment or strategic decision. Per Phil Fisher (Common Stocks and Uncommon Profits), "What counts is knowledge of background conditions. An understanding of what probably will happen over the next several years is of overriding importance...[I]t is the next five years' earnings, not those of the past five years, that now matter."

- FROM CHAPTER 1 -

ADDITIONAL POINT: WILL INCOMES CONTINUE TO RISE IN CHINESE CITIES?

This is an important Question. In fact, much of this book is predicated on incomes continuing to rise. But the real answer is yes and no.

The first twenty years of China's urbanization were all about GDP growth, which had some inevitable impacts on employment. Lots of people moved from farms to the cities and got jobs. But the excess labor from the countryside resulted in relatively modest income growth. GDP grew faster than income. Today, wage growth is picking up and with it income. But the relationship between GDP growth and income has been tenuous thus far.

This topic tends to raise the question as to whether China is at the so-called Lewis Turning Point. A newly-industrialized country typically grows very fast by combining foreign technology, capital and cheap, relatively unskilled labor. But eventually wages increase and companies become less profitable. At that point (the Lewis Turning point), they need to find other sources of productivity growth. The macro-argument is that China is probably getting close to this point in many industries.

However, an increasingly urban environment also enables services. Medicine, finance, education and other professional services all depend on urban environments and urban professionals. Today, there are nowhere near enough professionals to meet growing demand for such services and it's not uncommon to see year-on-year salary increases of 30% in this space. A combination of tightening supply and booming demand translates into income growth for those who can find such employment.

The differences in incomes in big vs. small cities also matters. It's possible to make a case for Nike to stay in Portland rather than move to say, Los Angeles. The schools are good, housing is cheaper, there is lots of green, etc. It's a lot harder for Anta, the local Jinjiang footwear champion, to make a similar case to its designers. They really don't want to live in a second tier Chinese city. Bigger cities are much better in China and this plays out in company behavior and the labor market. And big cities also get first dibs on everything from social life to foreign investment to tax incentives. It's hard for a small city to compete so the income question gets complicated here too. This big vs. small difference is bigger in China than in Europe or the US.

Overall, the question of rising incomes is important but pretty complicated. We are generally optimistic but it's complicated and something we leave to the economists.

China's urban income distribution will continue to widen

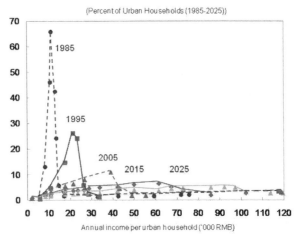

(Percent of Urban Households (1985-2025))

Annual income per urban household ('000 RMB)

Source: McKinsey & Co.

ADDITIONAL POINT: CHINESE RESTAURANTS ARE A FRAGMENTED AND STILL DEVELOPING INDUSTRY

According to Harvard Business Review and Freedonia Group, in 2010, the restaurant and contract food service industry in the USA was a $600 billion industry, with about 960,000 locations. Multi-unit concepts, like McDonalds, were about 30% of the market and the rest was individual operators. Even giant McDonalds only had about 3% of the total revenue for the US market. The restaurant situation in China is largely consistent with this, a mostly fragmented industry with shifting market share.

In the US, multi-unit concepts are mostly in three categories: specialty establishments like Starbucks and Dunkin Donuts; quick service restaurants like McDonalds and

KFC; and casual dining restaurants like Olive Garden and Applebees. For these categories, the prices step up correspondingly from under $5, to $5-10 to >$10.

However, in China independent full-service restaurants still dominate the market. These are the well-run, full-service, massive menu, excellent food restaurants that are a deep part of Chinese culture. And they have been around for thousands of years. In 2009, there were about 2.8M of these independent full-service restaurants. And they vary from high price to very low price. Unlike in the US, full-service restaurants and street vendors can both be at a lower price than fast food.

Quick service restaurants like McDonalds are a relatively new class of restaurants in China. They differentiate on convenient locations, a limited menu that is branded, vertical integration and a consumer brand that stands for reliability. These are somewhat sticky attributes so you don't see as much market movement in QSR. Once quick service enters a neighborhood, there is a race for locations, something that McDonalds is good at. But after that you do see leadership within quick service in a given territory. Tying up real estate does tend to stabilize market share. That is good news for companies like McDonalds and KFC.

ON FRAGMENTED INDUSTRIES IN DEVELOPING ECONOMY-STATE CAPITALISM

Fragmented industries are common in both developed and developing economies. There are lots of factors that can limit scale and keep an industry this way. Some are economic such as high transportation costs, personalized services (i.e., baby sitters), highly customized products, local operations (i.e., real estate brokers, auto repair), creative content (i.e., designers) and diverse customer types. Some factors that cause fragmentation are non-economic, such as government (licenses, labor rules, etc.)

As mentioned in the Appendix for the Introduction, just because the market is fragmented and you have small market share does not mean you can't make big profits. We have implied market share is a prerequisite for profits and an attractive ROIC. However, small companies can make significant profits. What matters is competitive advantage and how you define your market. If you are the only gas station in a small town, you can do quite well.

In China, fragmented industries are often because an industry is just developing. This makes sense in a developing economy. Either the market is just emerging because a product or service is now affordable. Or the industry is just developing the capabilities and degree of specialization necessary to deliver that type of product or service. So you want to distinguish between fragmented industries in the short-term and long-term. Certain aspects are inherently local and fragmented (local operations). Other aspects (marketing, food safety, R&D) are centralizable and become scalable over time.

An interesting phenomenon you do see in developing economies is a new industry or market will emerge and everyone will jump into it. You see a herd effect that is much greater than in the West. And then the players will all add scale at an alarming rate and usually drive the industry to massive over-capacity. In our last book, we described this as "Last Man Standing". Everyone scales up until the biggest player makes a tiny profit and everyone else bleeds cash. The last person standing when the dust settles gets the industry. If you are going to play Last Man Standing, you had better be sure if the industry is not fragmented in the long-term.

The most important lesson is, of course, don't try to dominate an industry if the economics are inherently fragmented. You will most likely end up spending money that others will then match. And the total value creation will be zero or negative. You are often better off staying small, trying to build a competitive advantage and pulling out what cash you can.

ON OPERATIONAL EFFECTIVENESS IN DEVELOPING ECONOMY-STATE CAPITALISM

Competitive situations without a competitive advantage are well-known and well-studied. The most well-known approach is probably Michael Porter's discussion of the productivity frontier in the Harvard Business Review. There are some important differences between that framework and our description of an Operational Marathon.

For those who aren't familiar with the Porter framework, the idea is that absent a set of unique activities that creates a competitive advantage, you are basically doing the same set of activities as every other company (i.e., no competitive advantage). So you can forget strategy. You compete by who can do those same activities the most effectively. That means being efficient, deploying capital smartly, managing labor, developing products quickly, effectively selling and a long list of other activities that move you towards creating greater value out of a set of cost inputs. There is arguably a productivity frontier (shown below) where it is not possible to get more value or a lower cost out of the business. And competition by companies pushes this frontier forward over time. But as no company has an advantage over another beyond operational effectiveness (i.e., management performance), you get absolute but not relative productivity increases. The industry and customers do better. But no individual competitor does.

If you have a competitive advantage then you are doing different activities (per Porter, activities are "the unit of competitive advantage"). You are doing something others cannot. Per Porter, it is best if have 4-5 activities that others cannot do and that they are all intertwined (i.e., a strategic fit). That makes them especially hard to copy. And even better is when such activities require trade-offs. You cannot do one without giving up on another activity. For example, full-service hub-and-spoke airlines cannot do low-cost airline activities without it hurting their core business.

However, in China (and other developing economies) we rarely talk about the productivity frontier. We are in a developing economy so we are not at global best practices or even close to the productivity frontier. Most developing economy business is about doing the basics and doing them cheaply. It is about efficiency , scale and the diffusion of technology. Absent a competitive advantage, you usually win (or survive) by being cheaper and bigger. Think about China Vanke building basic simple apartments cheaply and in great volume (over 80,000 per year). Or Haier building washing machines with acceptable quality and low cost. It has been mostly a game of scale and cost thus far.

China vs. Michael Porter's productivity frontier

Source: Adapted from Michael Porter / Harvard Business Review article

This is because operating at the productivity frontier in China is actually not possible. You don't have advanced management. You don't have specialized suppliers. You don't have developed infrastructure. And there is a limit to what technology you can actually deploy to increase productivity. Trying to deliver along the productivity frontier in China is like trying to race a Formula One car in the desert. The most surprising advice you often get in

China is "don't be so smart". Basically, don't try to maximize productivity and capture lots of little specialized efficiencies. Don't try to use the most advanced technology. Just do the basics well and cheap - and try to get big fast (which is how you get most of your cost savings). This is normal for developing economies. You can make a lot of money just by having solid management (which is actually rare) and doing the basics well. After that, you try to deploy proven technology as you can without making the situation unworkable.

So our Operational Marathon is a simplification of effectiveness to focus on speed and efficiency – and usually scale. Not productivity per se. In addition, China is a rapidly growing economy with emerging industries, so there are other reasons for going for speed and scale.

This situation has changed somewhat in the last 2-3 years. Some industries are maturing, growth is slowing and profits are shrinking for some. Given slowing revenue and rising input costs, it is about doing more with less (i.e., productivity). We have seen an increased shift from simple growth and efficiencies to productivity by other (usually more difficult) means. If the China game before was about being the biggest, in many industries it is now about being the smartest. The gap between China and the productivity frontier has shrunk. Much of the low hanging fruit is gone. A lot of the cross-border M&A currently in the newspapers is about acquiring technology, becoming smarter and closing this productivity and effectiveness gap.

- FROM CHAPTER 2 -

ADDITIONAL POINT: COMMERCIAL VERSUS STRATEGIC SOES

Some SOEs are basically commercial entities. In this book, we call them commercial SOEs. Some are active agents of the State. We call them strategic SOEs. And in between there is a lot of grey. Government ownership and/or control is a pretty complicated situation that doesn't lend itself to generalizations. You really have to look at the individual companies and industries. It is also worth pointing out that the State does not just mean the government. It can mean the government or the Party or both.

We will make a couple of other general comments about SOEs. But take these with a huge grain of salt. First, there are a lot of them. There are about 110 large SOEs directly controlled by the Central Government through the State-owned Asset Supervision and Administration Commission. However, the total number of subsidiaries at various levels under these SOEs is about 30,000. Plus there are lots of non-Central SOEs, controlled by local governments.

Second, management teams of SOEs usually have different interests than managers with private owners. There is often not a lot of focus on profits and earnings. And executives at SOEs have mixed and often unclear incentives regarding how they handle company assets.

Third, size is usually the primary management goal. There is a pursuit, sometimes blindly, to get bigger. One SOE chairman said there are only two rules for SOEs: 1) do real estate; 2) get bigger. So there is lots of M&A. There is also lots of jumping into other industries. The unsurprisingly leads to the creation of conglomerates. It is growth for growth's sake.

Fourth, many commercially-focused SOEs are poorly managed relative to private companies. But they do, as mentioned, often have other strengths that can compensate. For example, they can do acquisitions quickly, especially if they are buying other SOEs. They can sometimes access cheap bank loans, which most private companies cannot. They can get regulatory approvals faster. They usually have advantages in securing concessions, construction contracts, and legacy assets.

This is mostly because state agencies tend to help SOEs and SOEs tend to trust and help other SOEs (more than private companies). And the senior management of SOEs and government agencies seem to all interchange every 3-4 years, often going from company to regulator and back again. They are all basically the same group of people and who you know matters. That is a huge generalization but take it as directionally true for this discussion.

So in a business like mining or real estate where it is about doing lots of transactions, getting land, getting debt and getting approvals, commercial SOEs can do quite well. For example, in the dairy sector, SOEs dominate. Even though food scandals should give foreign companies an advantage, it is state-owned China Food, Bright Dairy and Yili that are now the largest. However when it comes to running restaurants and other operationally complex businesses, they tend not to do as well as the private companies.

Fifth, Chinese SOEs tend to acquire private competitors with a "wait and strike" approach (a term by author Joe Zhang). This usually happens when a private company hits an industry downturn and an SOE buys them up. And often, private companies find life much easier when they have an SOE parent. They move into the EZPass lane. A good example of this was China Food's acquisition of Mengniu. State Pharma Group has also been making private acquisition after acquisition. All of this affects the competitive dynamics.

Sixth, one downside to SOEs interest in M&A is they are not always terribly concerned with financial performance. A government audit of the 2012 books of 11 large state-owned firms found significant problems in their investments. Acquisitions and joint ventures were frequently done without appraising the actual assets. They were frequently done without feasibility studies, approvals from their boards or approvals from the NDRC. Unsurprisingly, many SOEs later book large losses on their acquisition activity.

ON COMPETITIVE ADVANTAGE IN DEVELOPING ECONOMY-STATE CAPITALISM

Virtually every company talks about their competitive advantage but very actually have one. And even fewer have one that lasts. Most companies are in operational marathons and are continually fighting to increase their size, their resources / assets, their capabilities, their efficiencies and lots of other things.

But a select few companies have real competitive advantages that create a serious barriers to entry and limit their competition. When asked by a student at Columbia Business School what was the one thing he would want to know about a company if he could know only one thing, Warren Buffett replied "whether it has a sustainable competitive advantage".

As a quick review, competitive advantages are usually described as one of four types:

1. Captive customers (i.e., a revenue advantage)

- The company can charge more because of significant switching or searching costs. Or because they are part of the habits of their customers (hello Starbucks). Having captive customers lets you increase pricing (somewhat) without losing them to competitors or new entrants. So a revenue advantage shows up as abnormally high profits (usually in gross profits), and hopefully against invested capital as well.

- Per Warren Buffett (Financial Crisis Inquiry Commission, 2011), "The single most important decision in evaluating a business is pricing power. If you've got the power to raise prices without losing business to a competitor, you've got a very good business. And if you have to have a prayer session before raising the price by 10 percent, then you've got a terrible business."

2. A production advantage (i.e., a cost advantage)

- The company can make things cheaper because they have proprietary technology or lower costs of inputs or some sort of special resource or location. This is typically in manufacturing or technology fields. But it could be as simple as having the only granite quarry in town (granite is expensive to transport long distances). Either way, it translates into a low cost production advantage and your profits again are abnormally high.

- In China, this is more common than in the West, and also in a different way. In the West, this is mostly about intellectual property or technology. The other types of production advantages (access to low-cost labor, resource access, etc.) tend to fade quickly in freer markets.

- However, in China, having a unique production advantage can last for a long time. State-related capabilities are definitely important here (discussed below). As is what happens to legacy state assets. Resources (minerals, land, and water) can be particularly difficult to access and expensive in many parts of China.

- Another big example would be capital advantages. Larger companies, especially SOEs, raise and deploy a lot of capital cheaply. So they can often more easily and cheaply buy land, buy resources, build factories, do R&D, and build brands. These large capital outlays can be a short-term barrier to entry against the vast sea of smaller, really hard-working and mostly private Chinese companies.

3. Economies of scale (i.e., a cost advantage)

- This is most of the situation discussed in beer. You have economies of scale relative to the local market that lets you beat much smaller competitors on per unit costs within a set time period. For this you need a business with significant fixed costs. These can be marketing, R&D, production, distribution or other activities. And you need to be much bigger than others relative to the market volume, so you have an advantage on per unit costs. It's a volume effect within a certain period of time. Both the fixed cost and scale conditions are necessary.

- And you have to actively defend against new entrants. This advantage doesn't mean much if the management isn't using it to hurt smaller competitors. This is a big deal in China, especially given the scale some players have in manufacturing and sales and distribution (China is a big country to cover).

- Cumulative experience is a related barrier that we don't really talk about much in China. The idea is that you accumulate so much internal expertise over time that you can produce a product or service at a lower cost in labor-intensive industries. It's not a volume effect like economies of scale. It's more of a cumulative effect. This is not as common in developing economies. And you don't see a lot of focus on these intangibles - like brands, process standardization (BYD for example) and research. This is partly because products and services are still relatively basic. And partly because IP and other intangibles are easily copied and stolen. You can find exceptions like investment banks and creative groups that have unique cultures (Jorge Lemann in Brazil). But people mostly tend to focus on more tangible things such as capital, distribution and economies of scale. But the difference between scale and experience is important to note.

- Access to distribution channels is particularly important in China. Distribution is so fragmented and in many cases so underdeveloped (third and fourth tier cities, inland China), that access becomes a major part of competition. This can be at the wholesale and retail level for consumer products. Snow, the number one beer in China, owes a lot of it success to the massive distribution of its owner China Resources.

- You could consider the network effect a type of economies of scale (i.e., lower unit costs). But that feels like a stretch so we'll just consider it a separate thing (discussed in the chapter on auctions).

4. Government as a Competitive Advantage

- This tends to be a catch-all bucket of government granted competitive advantages. Usually strategy books give you a list of things such as patents, regulations, tariffs and quotas, subsidies and taxes, purchase preferences and so on. And as mentioned, these often get buried within other factors (regulations increase costs which help incumbents, cheap loans help state-connected players, etc.).

- However, we define government as a competitive advantage only when it is a hard barrier to entry. That means licensure or other serious limits to market entry. This is a much narrower definition. This is frequently seen in strategic SOEs such as Baosteel, China Mobile and PetroChina. However, such government-granted competitive advantages can be given to private companies, foreign companies, commercial or strategic SOEs and to various types of JVs. It is worth noting that while strategic SOEs are sometimes protected by a high barrier to entry but they are also often forbidden from exiting (a high exit barrier). This results not only in under-supply (which we like) but also often in oversupply (hello steel industry).

- The other often-listed government factors such as access to resources, easier partnerships with local governments, tax credits, loan support and favorable regulation are not hard barriers to entry. So we do not consider them competitive advantages.

206

We consider them under regulations, State-related capabilities, and State-related assets - which mostly impact ongoing competitive dynamics, and do not overtly shape the industry or competitive structure itself. Regulations and rules are a bit of a mix. They can shape industry structure and at a certain point they do increase the capital costs of entry to the point of a significant barrier. We discuss these other factors in Chapter 4.

- At first pass, government as a real competitive advantage is simple. If the Chinese government says only China Mobile and China Unicom can have mobile licenses, then there is no other competition. End of story. If the US government says you must have bonds rated by one of only three companies (Moodys, S&P and Fitch), then competition is limited to three. So it can be a very strong and simple competitive barrier. But these advantages are also unpredictable. Political rules that protect you can be changed at any time (live by politics, die by politics). Commercial competitive advantages typically decline over time based on economics. Government competitive advantages tend to change abruptly and often as step-wise functions.

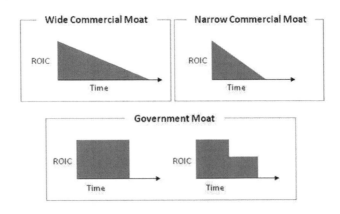

All of these things prevent competitors from entering. So your market share is hopefully stable over time (i.e. nobody can take customers from you). And you can get away with making bigger profits, relative to capital deployed, without being undercut by competitors. For example, the only restaurant in the airport terminal can raise prices because there is nowhere else to eat. The largest battery maker in China can make cell phone batteries cheaper than anyone else. Ultimately, a competitive advantage needs to show up as stable market share and an abnormally high ROIC-WACC. Otherwise you probably don't have one.

ON MATURING INDUSTRIES IN DEVELOPING ECONOMY- STATE CAPITALISM

A final question is what will happen when we finally reach steady state in Chinese beer. The growth rate has already fallen to around 5% and the market has mostly consolidated to 4-5 giants. So the question is is there anything that could change or disrupt a stable giants and dwarves situation? Could market share be shifted? Could a new entrant disrupt the situation? Could the State become more involved? And will the steady-state giants be profitable relative to capital?

This seems to be the question Warren Buffett has spent his life studying (well except for the State part). His focus is often on industries where the market is predictable and the winners are already known (at least to him). And then he assesses the sustainability of their competitive positions, profits and investor returns. Typical questions might be:

- Is there a potential technological disruption? Buffett famously got his friend Bill Gates to admit there was nothing he could do to disrupt the chewing gum industry. There is likely little risk of major technological disruption in beer.

- Is the situation dependent on good management? In the case of beer, we would say yes. Local economies of scale need to be actively defended. If someone enters your market, you need to prevent them from getting to your size (at which point you lose your advantage).

- How will the company fare under adverse situations? If the economy collapses, will beer makers start losing money? What about an increase in the input costs? Can they increase prices to cover?

- Does the company have a share of the consumer mind? And could this change? Note that in spite of the recent food safety issues, 9 out of 10 of the leading food product brands in China are Chinese. Food scandals are important in operational marathons but appear to be no match for entrenched economies of scale.

This is all part of the larger question of how do industries mature in developing economy-State capitalism. The story of beer in China is really about this maturation process. The 1980's saw an explosion of breweries as everyone rushed into the sector. The process of consolidation over the past twenty years has really been about maturation. A couple of comments on this:

- We are now seeing slowing growth and increased focus on fighting for market share.

- We will see rationalization of the operating structure. There are too many plants in some places, a natural result of the growth and frenzy period.

- We are seeing more focus on cost structures. Competitors, buyers and suppliers are all looking at each cost item more. This will inevitably lead to a drop in profits across parts of the industry. You really want to be an entrenched giant before that happens.

One result of this maturation is that manufacturing, marketing, distributing, selling and research are becoming less about adding capacity and more about being more productive. Just coming up with new products is going to be harder than it used to. Selling is going to be harder.

Customers are more knowledgeable now and putting girls in beer outfits in bars won't work like it used to. There is going to be a drive toward efficiency and effectiveness.

All of this is good news for the beer giants. They already have the market share. They can focus on selling more to their current customers. And they have more time to focus on their cost structures, their plant efficiencies and maximizing their pricing. In contrast, all of this will be brutally painful for the dwarves. You can expect to see some distressed companies and the giants buying them up.

As China's overall economy slows, we can see this same maturation process happening in other industries. Industries that had rapid growth are beginning to tighten and profits are shrinking. There will be more fighting for shrinking dollars - as well as well as increased battles with suppliers and buyers. Entire industries will try to wring out the excess profits. And those industries with above normal profits will likely be hardest hit (absent a competitive advantage).

A final point. In the last chapter we talked about how hard an operational marathon can be. But you really don't want to be in an operational marathon in a maturing industry. That is even harder.

- FROM CHAPTER 3 -

ADDITIONAL POINT: GOVERNMENT'S FIVE EFFECTS IN DEVELOPING ECONOMY-STATE CAPITALISM

We have argued that three factors and questions are dominant in the fight for Chinese consumers. The first is "Does the company have a competitive advantage?" This is a well-understood question and we have discussed some of the differences in developing economy-State capitalism in the previous chapter Appendix. However, the second question "Is the State an active force?" does not have a clear framework. In fact, the role of the state and the uncertainties it creates is usually what gives most analysts trouble when looking at China business.

In our flow chart, we have put this second factor in the middle of the chart. And we have broken it down to very specific questions about State actions. However, this is really just the useable version of the framework presented in this section.

We argue that when the State is an active force it has five potential impacts on competition and industry structure:

1. Government-granted competitive advantages (frequently to strategic SOEs).

2. Direct involvement with strategic SOEs or other as competitors.

3. Regulations / rules for the industry – this also includes education and information to the public on State preferences.

4. State-related assets – such as land, loans, legacy assets (factories, operating platforms, etc.), tax credits, etc.

5. State-related capabilities – technology transfer, government approvals, contracts from SOEs, etc.

The first factor (government-granted competitive advantage) was discussed in the previous chapter Appendix and we refer you to that section.

For the second factor, government can have direct involvement with strategic SOEs or others as competitors. In the previous chapter, we put SOEs into two categories: commercial and strategic. Commercial SOEs, such as beer companies, can be competitors but this does not reflect the State as an active force. The market operates mostly commercially. However, with strategic SOEs the government is a player in the industry. How do you compete against China Mobile? Even if they don't have a competitive advantage (most don't), how do you compete with a company like Kunming Steel in Kunming? In these situations you can assume a couple of things:

- The rules and regulations are going to favor them – both in design and in implementation. SOEs are very good at knowing which rules they can ignore.

- The other industry participants, such as buyers and suppliers, are going to favor them, especially if they are also SOEs. And the local governments and State-owned banks definitely are going to favor them.

- The industry is going to operate with a mix of economic and likely non-economic rules and objectives. In some industries, like healthcare, the economics can be very political. In other industries, like steel, they can almost be non-sensual. A lot of this plays out through the actions of the strategic SOEs (such as public hospitals and government owned steel mills). If you are competing with a company that can operate non-economically, that impacts you.

FOR THE THIRD FACTOR, GOVERNMENT SETS REGULATIONS AND RULES FOR THE INDUSTRY.

This is pretty straightforward and is something those in the West are familiar with. There are three aspects of this that are different in developing economy-State capitalism that are worth pointing out.

First, the rules and regulations can change quickly. They do not follow a democratic process (which is usually slower) and they are set and can be changed at the central, provincial and local government level. Plus in China the policy doesn't actually have to change. Sometimes the enforcement and implementation will change. The government will ignore this rule or start to enforce that one.

Second, the rules can be applied differently to different types of companies. Sometimes the rules will be generally positive (e.g., encouraging growth or development of an industry). Sometimes the rules will be generally constraining (e.g., the industry employs a lot of people and stability is important). Sometimes they will explicitly or implicitly favor one type of company (foreign versus domestic, private versus SOE, a special economic zone versus regular market, a specific geography versus others, a customer type versus another, etc.).

Third, rule and regulation announcements are a type of education and information on State preferences and objectives. This is very important. The more you think of the State as a player shaping some industries and not a bunch of sub-factors in a 5 forces economic structure, the more it makes sense to listen to what the State is saying. In China, the State will usually telegraph its moves and be clear about its objectives (development vs. growth vs. profit vs. employment vs. stability etc.) in a sector. So rules and regulation are a very important type of education and information for the public on State preferences. Chinese companies in particular are very good at understanding the State's goals and the explicit versus implicit rules.

FOR THE FOURTH FACTOR, STATE-RELATED ASSETS AND RESOURCES CAN BE VERY IMPORTANT IN ONGOING COMPETITION.

You can look at competitive dynamics and industry structure as the result of various forces (mostly economic) playing out over the long-term. Or you can look at them as the accumulations of differing capabilities and assets among competitors. If everyone has the similar capabilities and assets, then competition is mostly about operational execution (Operational Marathon). If a few companies have superior assets or capabilities, then they are doing different activities and could have a competitive advantage. A competitive advantage can equally be described as the summation of various forces, a set of differing activities or the result of the accumulation of superior capabilities or assets. The overall industry structure tends to be easier to understand by various forces. But ongoing dynamic competition, especially in a developing economy, tends to be easiest to view as a fight for capabilities and assets by various companies.

Assets and resources that relate to the State can be decisive in this type of ongoing competition. Such assets can include land, state-backed loans, legacy assets (such as state-owned factories and breweries), tax credits (also capital), etc. For Chinese consumer-facing businesses, financing, land and factories are usually the largest State-related assets. As mentioned, the historically State-owned breweries of China were a major factor in the ongoing competition in the beer space. And if you get into the B2B and industrial space, State-related assets are a really big thing.

It always worth looking at the various assets on the balance sheets of SOEs and companies in an industry, especially if it is an emerging or developing industry. The question we have put in the flow chart is are these State-related assets decisive in competition? As they were in beer.

FOR THE FIFTH FACTOR, STATE-RELATED CAPABILITIES CAN ALSO BE IMPORTANT IN ONGOING COMPETITION.

This is similar to the previous factor but more intangible. State-related capabilities can include technology transfer, government approvals, an ability to get contracts and concessions (say from SOEs and local governments), being the beneficiary of government research divisions (not insignificant in the technology sector), access to distribution and so on. These factors also tend to play out in competition over the longer-term. You can view the discussed EZPass effect as an example of this. This State-related capability is currently playing in private equity, where domestic firms can close deals in two weeks but foreign private equity firms require 2-3 months for government approvals. Distribution of consumer products through SOEs can also be very important State-related capability in B2C.

***

We will refer to these five factors throughout the book. Factors 1-3 tend to directly shape the industry structure. With a government-granted competitive advantages being the most clear form of this (e.g., three companies have government-granted licenses). This effect is often well-known very early on. For factor 2, strategic SOEs as competitors can also be decisive in industry structure and can happen very quickly. The discussed Poly Auctions was only launched in 2005 but quickly dominated Chinese auctions. For factor 3, rules and regulations are more dynamic and can be decisive or insignificant in industry structure. This is something that is followed on an ongoing basis and is usually the biggest source of uncertainty.

Factors four and five tend to play out in competition over time. And they are much more predictable. You can see assets and capabilities being accumulated over time, regardless of government rules or objectives. And as most dynamic competition is ultimately about how management uses assets, resources and capabilities we have described them with the same terminology. State-related capabilities and assets can play out in a powerful way among competitors who have management teams with different levels of ability. These two factors are relatively predictable.

Overall, factors 1, 2, 4 and 5 tend to be predictable in the medium-term. And if there is a strong consumer presence and if you can get a clear answer on competitive advantage, then you can be fairly confident about what is going to happen.

Let us reiterate an earlier point. These five factors can all be placed within various economic forces. But if you view developing economy-State capitalism as significantly about players and their self-interests (and not rational economics over the long-term), then you are often far better pulling out government as a powerful force in itself. And often with a clear self-interest and multiple lines of implementation for those interests. That is the right side of our consumer pyramid and that is why our second question is whether the State is "active force". To not view government as an active player with a mix of interests in those situations is to miss the forest for the trees.

There is a lot more to State capitalism than those five factors. Indeed, how competition and competitive advantage differs in developing economies and State capitalism is one of Jeff's big obsessions in life. But we think these five factors plus the China consumer pyramid are a good framework for the cases we have presented. These are micro-models that can be helpful in many, but not all, situations.

ADDITIONAL POINT: CHINA CAN GENERATE HUGE RETURNS FOR THOSE THAT WORK WELL WITH THE STATE

Two Chinese (Poly, Guardian) and two international (Christie's, Sotheby's) auction houses are now starting to compete. And they are both targeting affluent Chinese consumers. This is one of those situations where even though the competitive dynamics are clear (Giants, Dwarves and the State), the outcome is somewhat unpredictable. This is due to the cross-border nature of much of the competition. But it is also because it depends on the behavior of the individual companies.

COMPETITION BETWEEN ART AUCTIONS IS USUALLY ALL ABOUT THE NETWORK

Typically, the competitive advantage of auction house is its network of buyers and sellers. If you have a rare and valuable piece of art, you only want to sell it at Sotheby's or Christie's because that is where all the largest buyers are. Sotheby's in particular is known for its ability to access the world's 150 top art buyers. Auction houses benefit from the network effect, which is valuable for predicting auction pricing in particular. In China, we see a regional version of this same network effect. Plus the Chinese giants have direct government involvement and support so that is another type of competitive advantage. So in this situation, all four giants have impressive competitive advantages.

The question is how will these four auction giants behave towards each other? Will they start price wars and have big market share but little profit? Will they avoid direct competition by focusing on different geographies or art types? There are lots of examples of giants prospering together. And there are lots of examples of giants making life miserable for each other. What is different in this case is we have the State as a major player. That changes the expectations regarding behavior.

WHAT WOULD JOHN NASH DO?

How giants behave toward each other is a subset of the larger topic of economic vs. behavioral decision-making and game theory. Nobel Laureate John Nash showed that multiple such parties could reach stable equilibria through non-cooperation. The example of this was shown in the movie A Beautiful Mind was when five guys in a bar each decided not to compete for the prettiest girl. Instead they each asked out a not-as-pretty girl (everyone pursues their own best interest, while being aware of the strategies of the others).

The problem in "Giants, Dwarves and the State" is we really don't know how the giants are going to behave.

Some giants are purely commercial. Some are acting more strategic. And the State's interest is non-economic. So how do you game that out? How would you avoid needless confrontation and maximize the benefit across this situation? That would be a good question for John Nash.

It appears today that the Chinese government is actively managing the Chinese art industry and the competitive dynamic. It is definitely protecting Chinese art. And by allowing foreign giants to enter and compete for local business, it is increasing the supply of Chinese art into the country. But it is also probably "putting crocodiles in a pond". By allowing foreign competitors into the market, the local auction houses will have to become more professional and competitive.

Our point is that management behavior is a critical part of Giants, Dwarves and the State. And we can look to the pharma and auto sectors for examples. In those cases, what you see is that private companies that work in collaboration with the State can make tremendous returns. That is probably the biggest take-away from this situation. It can be exceptionally profitable. But that depends on working with the State and understanding the behavior of the giants.

However, such unpredictability is not unique to China. Per Charlie Munger, Vice Chairman of Berkshire Hathaway: "Many markets get down to two or three big competitors—or five or six. And in some of those markets, nobody makes any money to speak of. But in others, everybody does very well. Over the years, we've tried to figure out why the competition in some markets gets sort of rational from the investor's point of view so that the shareholders do well, and in other markets, there's destructive competition that destroys shareholder wealth."

- FROM CHAPTER 4 -

ADDITIONAL POINT: ON EMERGING VERSUS MATURING INDUSTRIES IN DEVELOPING ECONOMY-STATE CAPITALISM

The potential transition of deathcare from a Treadmill to a growing and / or developing industry (Operational Marathon; Credit-Fueled Sprint; Giants, Dwarves and the State; etc.) is a subset of larger question. How do industries emerge in developing economy-State capitalism?

In Western markets, there is lots of good thinking on this subject. Usually it is about a new business model or technology. If it is a new technology creating a new industry (the Internet, smartphones) or disrupting an old one (self-publishing), the question is usually about choosing the right technology (will GSM or CDMA be adopted?) or business model. It is also a lot about watching for consumer switching. Do consumers switch to the substitute (Netflix instead of Blockbuster).

In China and in other developing economies, emerging industries are rarely about technology. Occasionally, a company like Tencent will create a completely new mobile phone app but most companies (even the technology ones) are about bringing proven technologies or business models from the West into China. Hence the name developing economies. The main issues for emerging consumer industries in China are usually rising consumer wealth, the role of the State and infrastructure. We already know that dental implants and in vitro fertilization are going to emerge in China. We already know pretty much what the industry structure is going to look like when it does. And we know what the technologies are going to be. When we talk about technology in China, we are usually talking about "new to China" technology. It already exists elsewhere. What we don't know is at what point consumers can afford this (and want it), can it be deployed and how the State will react.

The first issue for emerging consumer industries is consumer wealth. As Chinese consumers rise in wealth, certain products and services become affordable. An example of this would be specialized medical services. You can now see Chinese consumers showing up in Los Angeles for IVF treatments by the thousands. And you can see dental labs offering implants and other higher-end cosmetic services exploding across China. That take-off point has been reached.

But the role of the State is a key factor. IVF is political and the regulations are complicated. Especially because IVF licenses can only be held by hospitals, most of which are SOEs. And that is really what we were talking about for deathcare. Funeral services have long been affordable. And people were already being buried so the market was not emerging. The question was will the regulations and other roles of the State allow the industry to emerge? And how?

A third factor is infrastructure or some other required capability. In IVF and dental implants, a big problem is the lack of trained doctors and dentists. In many products in Western China, the problem is the lack of warehouses and other logistics. The infrastructure limits how you can supply as a product or service. Looking at the discussed cases, both McDonalds and Carlsberg were clearly emerging industries in the 1980's and 1990's. They both initially had fragmented markets as the businesses first rolled out. But the demand, consumer wealth, policies and infrastructure were already mostly there. The NBA and art auctions were more pure emerging industries. They did not exist as products in China before. And in both of these cases, it was rising consumer wealth and the role of the State that determined the rate of emergence.

If emerging industries are about uncertainty, you have more uncertainty related to the State in China but less uncertainties in technology, business model and industry structure. And if the State is actively supporting your attempt at development (say in electric cars today), then industries can actually emerge much faster than in the West.

Per our final point for this chapter, if an industry has failed to emerge there is probably a very good reason for it. And you should be skeptical about it happening this year. Usually industries fail to emerge because of the role of the State. Second to that you can see stagnant industries because of a lack of certain capabilities (a lack of dentists and doctors in healthcare), a lack of raw materials and an absence of infrastructure (a common problem Inland right now).

Another related point is that emerging industries in the West are often about disruption. They are about a technology or a service that is disrupting an existing market. However, in State capitalism, you are often disrupting the State and that doesn't go over very well. The picture we usually see is not Netflix versus Blockbuster. It is usually more like Uber fighting the taxi cartels and city governments. When you try to disrupt State capitalism, it is a lot more difficult than in free markets. Get your lawyers and lobbyists ready.

ADDITIONAL POINT: ON WINNING (OR AVOIDING LOSING) IN EMERGING INDUSTRIES IN DEVELOPING ECONOMY-STATE CAPITALISM

When a new industry emerges, there is often a stampede effect. Everyone starts running after the opportunity. This to some degree is the nature of developing economies. You often see lots of irrational investment, especially if the new industry is perceived as sexy or strategically important. Money floods the sector. Companies jump in. And it's an even bigger stampede if the government announces its intention to support that particular industry. This happens every six months in China. It is usually followed several years later by a painful rationalization, especially if the government has been funding development with cheap debt.

So the question is how do you win in an emerging industry in developing economy-State capitalism? Do you join
the stampede? Try to outspend everyone? Per our main
thesis, the two critical factors are competitive advantage
and the role of the State. Starting with competitive advantage, it is useful to note what competitive advantages are
typically not available in emerging industries.

- You are not going to get economies of scale in an
  emerging industry. This might happen in five years
  but not before then. Jonathan and I wrote about
  this in our last book and called this phenomenon
  Last Man Standing. You are not going to get a per
  unit cost advantage that matters early-on.

- Capital. Spending lots of money might scare off
  some competitors but there is a lot of money in
  China. This (and advertising) will help but it will
  not get you a barrier to entry.

- Brand. A big brand with lots of advertising may be
  required but is not going to be a barrier to entry.

What can work as a barrier to entry in emerging industries in China are the following:

- Access to distribution. This can be particularly
  powerful in China. The country is huge and infrastructure and distribution are a big problem. China
  Resources is very effective at using its national distribution to support its beer business. Alibaba has

been very good at using its control of online distribution to jump into new markets.

- Proprietary technology. In the West, this usually means patents. In China, you can actually do this effectively without patents or innovation. When Geely bought Volvo, it got complete models for cars that it could then build and sell in China. That remains an effective barrier and local car makers have still not been able to successfully build higher end cars (despite years of trying). Depending on the situation, you can have a technological barrier without IP and patents.

- Access to a unique resource. This typically doesn't work in the West. It can in China. It can work in raw materials. It can work in skilled labor. Many of China's manufacturers are currently trying to use their strengths in skilled labor (such as BYD) to take over new industries.

- A government-granted competitive advantage. This, of course, is the best. When the Internet was first introduced in China, the government granted about 10 licenses for internet cafes. If you had one of those, you did very well.

ADDITIONAL THOUGHTS ON OPERATIONAL MARATHON

1. COMPETITIVE ADVANTAGE

In this case, the absence of a competitive advantage / barrier to entry is paramount. Operational Marathon is an intense ongoing competition. Everyone is making lots of moves in terms of products, services and operations. Everyone is copying everyone. There is tons of undercutting of price. And there is frequent breaking of the rules.

This is Chinese hyper-competition. Most competitors have small market share but you can find this situation in consolidated industries as well. Profits tend to be small, but there are some exceptions to that. Fragmented does not always mean unprofitable. Per standard competitive strategy, competitive intensity tends to increase and be more price focused when there are more competitors (everyone cuts price cause they think nobody is watching), when there are high fixed costs, when there is under-utilized capacity, when everyone has same strategy, when product storage is expensive, when there are low switching costs, when there are lots of substitutes, and when there are high exit costs (strategically important industries, illiquid business with lots of assets, specialized equipment with low liquidation value, government limits on exits).

In the more common fragmented situation, there are lots of factors that can limit scale and keep the industry fragmented. Some are economic (doctors offices, hair salons, design studios, etc.). Some are from regulatory. Some are from other factors. The big factors to watch for in China related to fragmentation are new developing industries (beer in the 1980's), high transportation costs (logistics are a big deal in underdeveloped countries of China's size), high inventory costs, erratic sales and local government controls (i.e., farming). Per standard competitive strategy, other factors that are similar to those found in the West are businesses with personalized service, highly customized products, local operational intensity (i.e., McDonalds), creative content, diverse customer types, and situations where local image or brand is important. The main source of fragmentation that is common in the West that you don't see in developing economies is rapidly changing technology. There is much less disruption and much more catching-up to Western standards.

The more attractive positions in this "no competitive advantage" situation tend to be within small strategic groupings such as regional and local distribution platforms (you move lots of products), niche positions as a low cost alternative or niche customer foci with lots of operational intensity or personalization. The same strategies for dealing with fragmentation apply (de-couple the fragmented part, do lots of mergers/acquisitions, etc.). The key thing to keep in mind is that increasing scale likely doesn't' increase value (and will destroy value at some point.)

2. ROLE OF THE STATE

Government regulations and commercial SOEs are present but the State is not an active force according to our State framework.

3. MANAGEMENT PERFORMANCE AND BEHAVIOR

Ongoing management in this situation is very important. Frequently it is all-out war. And superior management performance over the long-term is critical (hence the name Operational Marathon). However, we have characterized this as a race for efficiency and scale in China. That is very different than how it would be described in the West, where it would be about overall effectiveness. This would include operating best practices such as productivity, research and development, sales, etc. It would be a far broader definition than just efficiency and scale. The playbook is simpler in China because the country is developing (far behind the productivity frontier) and more specialized and advanced performance is not possible. You don't do everything at best practice. You just do the basics well and fast.

There are some strategic (or tactical) decisions that matter. Given the competitive intensity, having a focused plan is critical. Management's plan for operational scale and efficiencies can also be viewed as the accumulation of certain assets and capabilities in a developing industry over time. This is a useful approach for developing economies. However, it is rare that these will ever be superior relative to competitors, just more of them. However, these assets / capabilities can sometimes become barriers at a certain point (discussed later).

4. EXTERNAL FACTORS

Consumer-facing markets in China tend to be high growth and volatile initially (i.e., emerging markets). Competitor behavior can frequently be irrational. Demand usually gets ahead of supply. And competitors can often view the industry as the new hot thing or a strategic necessity. It is often useful to look at behavior and interests more than economics for new consumer markets. In more mature China consumer markets, behavior is more rational and predictable economically.

A secondary external factor is technological advancement, which can be significant in some industries. We are not addressing this.

SUMMARY

Operational Marathon is overwhelmingly about ongoing operational competition against lots of rivals and new entrants – and often with a rapidly changing market. Behavior is mostly Darwinian.

ADDITIONAL THOUGHTS ON GIANTS AND DWARVES

1. COMPETITIVE ADVANTAGE

This is a more stable competitive structure where you don't have a lot of new entrants. And a couple of giants dominate the market and keep the dwarves small. So most of the attention is on the competition between giants, which can vary between sleepy behavior and all-out war. In many ways, this is similar to Giants and Dwarves situations in the West. More intensive competition tends to happen when 4-5 giants are all the same size. Or when there is lots of excess capacity or high fixed costs. Or when one player is just behaving erratically or stupidly. There is less competition when one company is much larger and the others all follow (leader-follower). Or when behavior is towards collaboration, or at least avoiding direct fights.

These situations are mostly commercial so these are typical competitive advantage questions. Barriers to entry can be on the customer side (switching costs, high frequency purchases, etc.) or on the supply-side (assets and cost barriers) or in operations (scale in sales and distribution, channel crowding, etc). You can view these as industry structures or ongoing asset and capability fights. You accumulate a competitive advantage or superior assets and capabilities over time. And you make sure smaller companies never get these.

However, in China we see a couple of important differences in this situation. The first is that behavior tends not to follow long-term economic models. It tends to follow the short-term self-interest of the players. It is more behavioral than rational or economic. This is especially true if commercial SOEs are present. Their interests tend to go towards growth and scale and less towards profits (let alone shareholder returns). And this growth and scale can often be done through mergers and acquisitions where they are known to pay scant regard to returns on capital. This situation is particularly acute if you are in a new or hot market that is just emerging.

A final point is to not underestimate the ability and willingness of some larger companies to jump over barriers to entry. Large companies with large resources, such as commercial SOEs and multinationals viewing this as a "must-win" market, will often use their size to bypass what appear to be significant barriers to entry.

2. ROLE OF THE STATE

Government regulations and commercial SOEs are present but the State is not an active force according to our State framework.

3. MANAGEMENT PERFORMANCE AND BEHAVIOR

This situation is mostly about the competition between the Giants. Management performance is more important in Operational Marathon. But behavior is important in Giants and Dwarves. This is a well-studied subject in the West (competition, collaboration, signaling, game theory, etc.). This is generally less predictable in developing economies. The markets are moving faster and the competitors are often less sophisticated. Price wars are more common. So is just inexplicable behavior. Combinations of economic and behavioral / interest-based decision-making are common.

4. EXTERNAL FACTORS

Consumer-facing markets in China tend to be high growth and volatile (i.e., emerging markets). Competitor behavior can frequently be irrational in response. Demand can get ahead of supply. But supply can also become excessive quickly. Especially when competitors view the industry as the new hot thing or a strategic necessity. It is often useful to look at behavior and interests more than economics. In more mature, usually slower growth China consumer markets, this tends to be a zero sum game and behavior is more rational and predictable economically.

A secondary external factor is technological advancement, which can be significant in some industries. We are not addressing this.

SUMMARY
This situation is mostly about ongoing direct competition and the relationship between the giants. There are few new entrants and minimal state involvement. Growing, changing and stabilizing market and customer demands are the other key factors to watch.

ADDITIONAL THOUGHTS ON GIANTS, DWARVES AND THE STATE

1. COMPETITIVE ADVANTAGE
This is a more stable industry structure, where you don't have a lot of new entrants and the dwarves are not a big threat. But competition between the giants depends on management behavior and the role of the State. So it is less predictable than Giants and Dwarves. More intense competition tends to happen when 4-5 giants are the same size. Or when there is lots of excess capacity or high fixed costs. There is less competition when one giant is much larger, State-backed or a strategic SOE - and the others are smaller (leader-follower). Or when behavior is towards collaboration, and not conflict.

These industries are a mix commercial and State goals. They can be economic, policy-based, interest-based or irrational. So competition is mostly the result of a mix of typical competitive advantages, State-granted competitive advantages, and the actions of strategic SOEs. Barriers to entry can be on the customer side (switching costs, high frequency purchases, etc.), on the supply-side (assets and cost barriers) or in operations (sales and distribution, channel crowding, etc).

You can view the industry as an ongoing asset and capability fight, which is helpful in this case. While state granted competitive advantages and regulations can be unpredictable, the accumulation of State-related assets and capabilities is predictable. This is an important and often unmentioned impact of the State on ongoing competition. It can shift the balance between giants and create new giants.

2. ROLE OF THE STATE

We argue that when the State is an active force it has five potential impacts on competition and industry structure:

1) **Government-granted competitive advantages** (frequently to strategic SOEs).

2) **Direct involvement with strategic SOEs as competitors.**

3) **Regulations / rules for the industry** – this also includes education and information to the public on State preferences.

4) **State-related assets** – such as land, loans, legacy assets (factories, operating platforms, etc.), tax credits, etc.

5) **State-related capabilities** – technology transfer, government approvals, contracts from SOEs, etc.

3. MANAGEMENT PERFORMANCE AND BEHAVIOR

Management behavior is critical. But the market is less predictable and less economic in nature in this case. Economic, policy and behavior-based decision-making tends to overshadow long-term economic forces. We see competition, collaboration, signaling and game theory as we see in the West. But we also see coevolution as government goals are often about development. Management behavior is more important in this situation. Management performance is more important in Operational Marathon.

4. EXTERNAL FACTORS

Consumer-facing markets in China tend to be high growth and volatile (i.e., emerging markets). Competitor behavior can frequently be irrational in response. Demand can get ahead of supply. But supply can also become excessive quickly. Especially when competitors view the industry as the new hot thing or a strategic necessity. It is often useful to look at behavior and interests more than economics. In more mature, usually slower growth China consumer markets, this tends to be a zero sum game and behavior is more rational and predictable economically.

A secondary external factor is technological advancement, which can be significant in some industries. We are not addressing this.

SUMMARY

This situation is mostly ongoing direct competition (no new entrants) and the relationship between the giants and the active role of the State. Growing, changing and stabilizing market and customer demands are the other key factors.

ADDITIONAL THOUGHTS ON STATE CARNIVAL

1. COMPETITIVE ADVANTAGE

This situation can vary between intense dynamic competition, rapid accelerations, industry-wide stagnation and chaos. In the absence of a competitive advantage or barrier to entry, everyone is making lots of moves in terms of products and operations. And there is usually tons of undercutting of price. Tons of copying. And there is frequent breaking of the rules.

Most competitors have small market share (depending how you define the market). And profits tend to be small, but there are some exceptions to that. Fragmented does not always mean unprofitable. You can also find some consolidated examples, but fragmentation is more common. Similar to standard competitive strategy, competitive intensity tends to increase and be more price focused when there are more competitors (everyone cuts price cause they think nobody is watching), when there are high fixed costs, when there is under-utilized capacity, when everyone has same strategy, product when storage is expensive, when there are low switching costs, when there are lots of substitutes, and when there are high exit costs (strategically important industries, illiquid business with lots of assets, specialized equipment with low liquidation value, government limits on exits).

In the more common fragmented situation, there are lots of factors that can limit scale and keep the industry fragmented. Some are economic (doctors offices, hair salons, design studios, etc.). Some are from regulatory and other factors. The big factors to watch for in China related to fragmentation are new developing industries (beer in the 1980's), high transportation costs (logistics are a big deal in an underdeveloped country of China's size), high inventory costs, erratic sales and local government controls (i.e., farming). Other factors that are similar to those found in the West are businesses with personalized service, highly customized products, local operational intensity (i.e., McDonalds), creative content, diverse customer types, and situations where local image or brand is important. The main source of fragmentation that is common in the West that you don't see in developing economies is rapidly changing technology. There is much less disruption and much more catching-up to Western standards. The other factors are mostly State-related (discussed in the next point).

The more attractive positions in this "no competitive advantage" situation tend to be within small strategic groupings such as regional and local distribution platforms (you move lots of products locally), niche positions as a low cost alternative or niche customer foci with lots of operational intensity or personalization. The same strategies for dealing with fragmentation apply (de-couple the fragmented part, do lots of mergers etc.). The key thing to keep in mind is that increasing scale likely doesn't' increase value (and will destroy value at some point.)

2. ROLE OF THE STATE

We argue that when the State is an active force it has five potential impacts on competition and industry structure:

1) **Government-granted competitive advantages** (frequently to strategic SOEs).

2) **Direct involvement with strategic SOEs as competitors.**

3) **Regulations / rules for the industry** – this also includes education and information to the public on State preferences.

4) **State-related assets** – such as land, loans, legacy assets (factories, operating platforms, etc.), tax credits, etc.

5) **State-related capabilities** – technology transfer, government approvals, contracts from SOEs, etc.

As discussed, this can be positive or negative. It can result in credit-fueled development, where you get lots of modernization, investment and supply. This often leads to profits but also non-economic thinking and oversupply. It can also be industry dysfunction and stagnation. You do lots of work but can't get anything done. Not only can't you build any competitive advantages, you often can't even accumulate assets and capabilities over time.

3. MANAGEMENT PERFORMANCE AND BEHAVIOR

Ongoing management is critical. It frequently means all-out war. It usually means trying to live in a non-economic industry. So performance is important for survival but may or may get you actual progress. Management behavior can vary between Darwinian and coordination.

4. EXTERNAL FACTORS

These are often stagnant markets. Demand can get ahead of supply but supply cannot often meet it. This shows up in things such as black markets and long lines out the hospital doors. Behavior is often irrational.

SUMMARY

This situation is mostly about ongoing direct competition and new entrants plus the active role of the State. Growing, changing and stabilizing State demands are the largest factor. Market and customer demands are usually secondary.

ADDITIONAL THOUGHTS ON WINNER TAKE ALL

1. COMPETITIVE ADVANTAGE

Life is good at the top. The biggest limitation is substitute products or services that can cap your pricing. In government-shaped markets, pricing can also be controlled. But there are no threatening rivals or new entrants and the biggest issue is the durability of the competitive advantage. Barriers to entry can be on the customer side (switching costs, high frequency purchases, etc.), on supply-side (assets and cost barriers) or in operations (sales and distribution, channel crowding, etc). You can view these as industry structures or an ongoing asset and capability fight. You accumulate dramatically superior assets and capabilities over time.

In the West, the biggest threat to this is typically technology changes. In China, a new State-backed competitor is the biggest threat. Or changes in policy directed at the winner. China's Internet leaders are particularly adept at managing their relationship with the State. These situations can be a mix economic and State-decided goals and industries can vary between purely commercial behavior and policy-based or interest-based behavior.

2. ROLE OF THE STATE
Can be lots of government or very little. But in this case the dominant competitive advantage overshadows this.

3. MANAGEMENT PERFORMANCE AND BEHAVIOR
Ongoing management is easy. The most important issue is defending the competitive advantage and managing the State relationship. Living and profiting in a non-economic industry can also be a challenge.

4. EXTERNAL FACTORS
These are usually more established markets, not a situation where multiple companies are going after a new opportunity. There is an established leader. Managing changing consumer demands is a key issue.

In some sectors, there are lots of technological issues.

SUMMARY

This situation is mostly about executing against growing or stabilizing market and customer demands. And secondarily about defending the competitive advantage and managing the relationship with the State.

28208918R00140

Made in the USA
Middletown, DE
07 January 2016